&

Grits

NATHALIE DUPREE'S
Shrimp & Grits
Cookbook

Nathalie Dupree's
Shrimp & Grits
Cookbook

Nathalie Dupree

with Marion Sullivan

Photographs by Chris M. Rogers

Wyrick & Company

Charleston

First Edition
10 09 08 07 06   5 4 3 2

Published by
Wyrick & Company
An imprint of Gibbs Smith, Publisher
P.O. Box 667
Layton, Utah 84041

Orders: 1.800.748.5439
www.gibbs-smith.com

Designed by Dawn DeVries Sokol
Printed and bound in Hong Kong

Library of Congress Cataloging-in-Publication Data

Dupree, Nathalie.
  Nathalie Dupree's shrimp & grits cookbook / Nathalie Dupree with Marion Sullivan ;
photographs by Chris M. Rogers.— 1st ed.
     p. cm.
  ISBN 0-941711-83-8
  1. Cookery (Shrimp) 2. Grits. 3. Cookery, American—Southern style. I.
Title: Nathalie Dupree's shrimp and grits. II. Title: Shrimp & grits. III.
Sullivan, Marion. IV. Title.
  TX754.S58D87 2006
  641.6'95—dc22
                              2005033875

Dedication

To Jack Bass and the Sullivan children

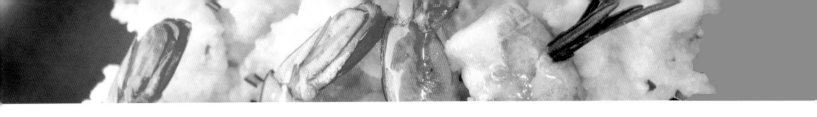

Contents

Shrimp and grits, one of the South's beloved foods, leaves a lingering taste and a folkloric mystique that borders on the mythical. Each community and ethnic group along the region's shorelines brings its own cultural influences to this dish.

A carriage driver in Charleston might tell visitors romantic tales about shrimpers heading out before dawn and using their catch for a tasty and nourishing early breakfast of shrimp and grits.

Others might imagine Native Americans bringing their corn to the Jamestown, Virginia colony and adding tiny local shrimp to their corn mush. No one really knows how the combination of shrimp and grits first came about.

We do know, however, that starting in early colonial days, many Carolina lowcountry inhabitants were dependent on fish and shrimp for food. Some form of grits have been around since before the Native Americans greeted the first white man with "rockahominie" (the Native American name for cracked corn; hence, we think, *hominy*). Grits are produced by grinding or pounding dried corn into pieces.

People who grew up on the South Atlantic and Gulf of Mexico coasts remember catching the tiniest and most flavorful of shrimp—"creek shrimp"—in the salt marshes and rivers and bringing them home to top their grits, unshelled, slathering everything with butter and pepper, and relishing them all together for breakfast. Perhaps they added a tad of hot sauce, or cooked up some country ham and made some brown sauce, or added some greens from last night's supper, and poured all that over the shrimp and grits.

Now, the crème de la crème of "New Southern" chefs combine grits, shrimp and a variety of ingredients from crisp bacon to finely chopped truffles, with more than fifty restaurants in Charleston, South Carolina, alone serving their own version of shrimp and grits. Some go so far as to grind dried corn and make their own grits or hominy. You'll find many of their recipes, easily done by the home cook, in this book.

Throughout much of the history of Southern cookery, grits have been eaten as a staple with a variety of seafood. Among the Jewish immigrants who settled in small Southern towns a century or so ago, some housewives served grits with fried salt herring, soaked overnight in water to leach out the brine, then fried in butter. My husband, Jack Bass, remembers this childhood dish as "delicious."

Grits are embedded in the region's bi-racial culture and celebrated in poetry, song, and story. There is even an annual grits festival in the town of St. George, South Carolina. An award-winning film, *It's Grits*, produced by South Carolina filmmaker Stan Woodward, captures the historic place of grits within the South's popular culture.

"Grits," says Southern food writer John Egerton in *Side Orders*, "are an all-purpose symbol for practically anything of importance to Southerners. They stand for hard times and happy times, for poverty and populism, for custom and tradition, for health and humor, for high-spirited hospitality. They also stand for baking, broiling, and frying. After a bowl of grits, we half expect to find the day brighter, the load lighter, the road straighter and wider."

While attending the St. George Grits Festival, I found all sorts of grinders for the fresh-milled corn, and purchased a number of different ones to use while testing these recipes. (I did not, however, join in the grits weighing contest, where contestants roll in a bathtub of cooked grits and then are weighed to see how much grits stuck to them.)

Various kinds of quick grits were used in testing recipes and developing this book. Most quick grits are lye-based. Others are freshly milled but are ground more finely and cook more quickly than stone-ground grits. Almost any grits can be ground finer in a food processor. No instant grits were used to test these recipes.

Nathalie Dupree
Charleston, SC

HOW SHRIMP ARE SOLD

While shrimp may be sold simply as small, medium, large, and jumbo at the seafood market or grocery store, the origin for these designations is a commercial grading system. The parameters are somewhat loose, but on average small has 50 to 60 shrimp to a pound, medium 36 to 50, large 21 to 35, and jumbo 16 to 20. The very biggest can be as large as 5 shrimp to the pound. When substituting a different size of shrimp in a recipe, check what size the recipe calls for and adjust the cooking time accordingly.

Most retail shrimp are sold headless. Occasionally, what looks like a bargain can be found: heads-on fresh shrimp at less

than half the headless price. However, the discarded weight of the heads will almost equal the higher price for heads-off and the purchaser or cook will have the task of beheading the shrimp. So it is probably no bargain.

The task of snapping off the head is worth it to many because fresh heads-on shrimp are one of the real treats of the sea. To tell just how fresh a shrimp is with a head on, look for its "whiskers" or antennae. They are prone to fall off as the shrimp ages more than a few hours off ice, or 12 hours or so after being caught. The heads are wonderful for stock and some people like eating the cooked head meat.

As for the sometimes black vein down the back of a shrimp, which is its digestive tract, some people see no need to remove the vein if they don't think it is sandy. Some chefs insist on having it removed with a pin, toothpick, or a plastic shrimp peeler that removes the shells at the same time.

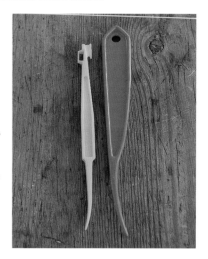

KINDS OF SHRIMP AND WHERE THEY COME FROM

Those who live on the shore consider fresh shrimp to be those which are not more than 12 hours old. Shrimp this fresh are considered a luxury food, whether you catch them yourself or buy them at a commercial shrimpers' dock. In the South, wild shrimp spawn in the saltwater marshes along the Carolina and Georgia coasts and along the Gulf shores. People with access to tidal creeks or marshes will go out during shrimp season with a seine or drop net and catch the small shrimp during their journey to the sea. These "creek shrimp" at their finest have a fragile, edible shell and a sweeter taste that aficionados prefer. When they have grown to the size of a thumbnail, the shrimp start to wind their way through the brackish sluices and marsh grass toward the saltwater where they will mature and grow.

Wild Gulf and South Atlantic Coast brown, pink, and white shrimp are among the finest in the world. These names don't clearly describe them, since most shrimp change color according to bottom type and water clarity. The scientific names are: Brown: Farfantepenaeus aztecus; Pink: *Farfantepeneus duorarum*; and White: *Litopenaeus setiferus*.

In addition, there is domestic shrimp farming and an abundant supply of imported frozen shrimp available throughout America.

Although commercial shrimp trawlers that go out of port for a week or more freeze shrimp, or refrigerate them on ice at a "near freezing" temperature as soon as they are caught, smaller trawlers land them fresh. Local purchasers buy them, heads on or off, right at the docks, at farmers markets, or from the back of a truck. Vacationers to the coast and locals alike stock up to freeze at home, because it is rare to find fresh shrimp for sale more than twenty miles inland.

METHODS FOR COOKING SHRIMP

Shrimp are wonderfully versatile when it comes to how they can be cooked. The key is to avoid overcooking, which results in tough and less flavorful shrimp. Once the shell begins to separate, usually in a minute of being placed in boiling water, remove, drain in a colander, and run cold water over them to stop the cooking process.

In addition to the traditional boil (technically "poaching," the heat being turned down as soon as the shrimp are added, since shrimp toughen if cooked at a hard boil), they can be sautéed, stir-fried, pan-fried, deep-fried, baked, steamed, cooked in beer or broth, broiled and grilled. Shrimp cooked any of these ways can be served over grits. Take the size of the shrimp into account; the larger they are the longer they cook. They can also be added peeled and without pre-cooking to a pot of grits or gravy for the last few minutes of cooking time. In fact, the add-to method has an extra benefit: it guarantees that every drop of succulent shrimp juice is locked right in.

If you prefer cooking the shrimp in the shell, as I do, you may simmer, sauté or grill the shrimp for a few minutes until

cooked, set aside, and add to a sauce at the end. Be sure to boil down the sauce before adding the cooked shrimp. If you simmer shrimp, this process will allow you to use the cooking water (stock) in the sauce.

COOKING GRITS

Grits are best added to boiling liquid in a slow steady stream, while being stirred constantly over a low heat. One cup of uncooked grits needs 4 cups of liquid and makes 4 cups of cooked grits. The measures may vary slightly according to the type of grits used, but liquid may always be added after they are cooked, or the lid taken off and the grits cooked down until the desired thickness. The liquids may be water, stock, milk, cream, or whatever else you can think of that would add the flavor and dimension to the final dish you are creating. Water and stock produce a less creamy result than milk and cream, but are easier to cook without scalding the bottom of the pan. Some people prefer their grits cooked "dry," meaning they will stand just where you left them when you dished them out; others prefer them "loose." It may have something to do with the way your mother cooked them.

No matter how slowly grits get added to the cooking liquid, or how well they are stirred, sometimes they lump. If lumps form, mash the grits against the side of the pan with a wooden spoon until broken up or, when cooked, rub through a flat slotted spatula or even a large-holed colander into a bowl. Push the large lumps through the holes. When cooked, keep completely covered. Plastic wrap put right on top of the grits will help prevent a skin from forming over them.

OTHER WAYS TO COOK GRITS

Cooking and clean-up is easiest, with the least risk of scorching, by cooking grits in the microwave in a heat-proof bowl. Only occasional stirring is required. Covering the bowl will speed the cooking, but may create steam that can cause a severe burn. Plastic wrap should have an open space for steam to escape, hot pads should be used, and removal from the bowl done with care, particularly if cooking half an hour or more. Time will vary according to the type and amount of grits. Instant and quick grits have directions on their packages. Stone-ground grits will vary from half an hour to an hour in the microwave. All time in the microwave is dependent on quantity, so a smaller quantity will cook more quickly than a large quantity.

John T. Edge has perfected the art of cooking stone-ground grits in a crockpot. They cook all night on very low heat, and in the morning they are piping hot and ready to eat for breakfast. We have also used electric rice cookers. Slow cookers, crockpots and electric rice cookers can work well, but may occasionally result in scorched grits if not watched. They should be stirred occasionally, which circumvents the problem. If this is not possible, just scoop off the brown part. Soaking grits overnight speeds the cooking the next morning.

Many people use a double boiler or "bain marie" (water bath) to cook their grits, finding that cooking them over water makes it easier to prevent scorching. Others use a "flame tamer," a little gadget that slows down cooking. A heavy pan is preferable, as is low heat, once the liquid has been brought to a boil as directed. Once again, cooking times vary according to the types of grits.

GRITS AND HOMINY

The early inhabitants of the Americas cultivated corn and learned how to deal with it, preserved and ground, cooked into mush-like mixtures. As far back as Plymouth, the Indians taught colonists how to refine corn to make it edible, using a giant mortar and pestle, which, according to scholar Betty Fussel, was called a samp mill, cracking the dried kernels to make meal or flour. ("Nasump," like "rocka-hominie," was an Indian word.) Water run through ashes makes lye, used in softening the hulls (skins) of corn kernels. Hominy stuck as a name, with no one much remembering

the word "sampe." Hominy was broiled, boiled, flattened, roasted over fire and made into breads and sweets.

In the South, we had "Big Hominy" and "Little Hominy." Big hominy was the lye-softened whole kernels, and little hominy was the skinned kernels that were ground. All over the South there were mills, frequently water driven, with large grinding stones below funnels into which the dry corn was fed. What came out of them after sifting, was called "stone-ground grits." Usually, the coarsest meal is called "grits," the next coarsest is "corn meal," and, finally, is soft "corn flour." Grits vary in nutrients depending on how much of the kernel and germ were saved in the grinding process.

Historically, Charlestonians persisted in calling it "hominy grits" (or gryts). This was produced, according to the owners of Anson Mills, by fresh milling corn, then winnowing out the hull to preserve whole corn nutrients, flavor and texture. Now the freshly ground corn is frequently just called grits. Anson Mills, and some few others, separates the fresh germ and meal from the coarse grits, and after sifting and cleaning, mixes them back in by hand, making a highly perishable product that must be refrigerated or frozen.

The Original Breakfast Shrimp & Grits

Serves 4

Originally entitled "Shrimps and Hominy" in the 1930 edition of *Two Hundred Years of Charleston Cooking*, this is the earliest recipe we could find. (It was changed to "Breakfast Shrimp and Grits" by the 1976 edition of the same book.) It was attributed to a man who said that he had been eating shrimp and hominy every morning for seventy-eight years during the shrimp season and never tired of it. Hominy was once the Charleston terminology used for cooked grits. We have cooked the grits in milk, although the recipe just called for "cooked hominy." You may peel the shrimp before or after cooking, but usually if people want to cook shrimp in the shell they simmer it rather than sauté it.

1 cup uncooked grits	$^1/_2$ cup (1 stick) butter
2-3 cups milk	Salt and freshly ground pepper
2 cups water	1 pound raw shrimp, shelled

Add the grits to simmering milk and water in a heavy saucepan, preferably nonstick, and cook as package directs, stirring constantly. Do not let the grits "blurp" loudly, and watch the evaporation of liquid. Add more if necessary. When fully cooked to the texture you desire, remove from heat and add 2 tablespoons of the butter and season with salt and pepper salt. Meanwhile, heat 4 tablespoons of the butter in a frying pan and sauté the shrimp in the butter until the shrimp turns pink. Add the rest of the butter to the pan and melt. Top the grits with the shrimp and pour the butter on top.

Variations:
Add 1 garlic clove, chopped, to the grits, and another to the shrimp.
Add 1 quarter-sized piece of ginger, chopped, to the shrimp when sautéing.
Sprinkle with chopped parsley, cilantro, basil, or thyme.

Starters & Soups

Asian-Style Shrimp and Crab Cakes

Makes 4 cakes as an appetizer

These cakes may be served as is for a starter or made smaller and passed at a party with small plates. In that case, omit the snow peas.

1/4 cup mayonnaise
2 tablespoons chopped fresh cilantro
1 tablespoon chopped peeled fresh ginger
2 teaspoons bottled Thai fish sauce (nam pla)*
   or soy sauce
1/3 pound cooked shrimp, peeled and chopped
1/3 pound crabmeat, gently picked over to
   remove any shell and drained of any liquid

2 tablespoons cooked grits, salted to taste
1 1/4 cups panko, divided*
Freshly ground black pepper
3 tablespoons peanut oil
1 cup snow peas, steamed and dried
Oriental sesame oil

Mix the mayonnaise, cilantro, ginger, and nam pla or soy sauce in a bowl. Mix in shrimp, crabmeat, grits, and half the panko. Season with pepper. Place the remaining panko on a plate. Drop one-fourth of the shrimp mixture into the panko, turn to coat, and shape into a cake 2 1/2 inches in diameter. Repeat coating and shaping with remaining shrimp mixture and crumbs, forming a total of 4 cakes.

Heat the peanut oil in a heavy-bottomed frying pan over medium heat. Add the cakes and sauté until crisp, about 5 minutes per side. Remove and drain on paper towels. Garnish the cakes with the snow peas, lightly drizzle sesame oil on top, and serve.

*These ingredients can be purchased at Asian grocery stores or the Asian section of many grocery stores.

Fried Grits, Shrimp and Tasso Logs

Serves 6 as a starter

These are fun to pass when serving beer or having a football party.

3 cups cooked grits, room temperature
2 tablespoons butter, melted
1/4 cup finely chopped tasso or smoked ham
1/4 cup chopped cooked shrimp
Salt

1/2 cup flour
2 eggs beaten with 2 tablespoons water
Dry fine bread crumbs
Vegetable oil

Combine the grits, butter, tasso, shrimp, and salt to taste. Spread out in an oiled 13 x 19-inch baking dish. Cool, cover, and refrigerate for up to 2 days.

Put the flour, eggs, and bread crumbs into separate shallow bowls. Cut the cold grits into twenty 4 1/2 x 1/2-inch logs. Roll the logs in the flour, then the eggs, and finally in the bread crumbs. Place the logs on a baking sheet and refrigerate, uncovered, for at least 1 hour, or overnight.

Fill a heavy-bottomed deep frying pan with oil approximately 1 1/2 inches deep, but no more than halfway up the sides. Heat the oil to 360 degrees F. Fry the logs in one layer, leaving enough space between to turn them, for approximately 1 minute, or until golden. Drain on paper towels and serve.

Grits with Greens and Shrimp

Makes 4 to 6 servings

If you find someone who doesn't swoon over this dish, don't bother cooking for them again. This is the kind of dish you lie in bed dreaming about and wishing you could have again. The heavy cream is a bit decadent, but that is why it is not an everyday meal. This is a special meal to serve to people who really love eating good food.

2 cups milk
2 cups water
1 cup grits
1 garlic clove, chopped
1 cup heavy cream
1/4 to 1/2 cup butter

1 to 2 cups freshly grated
    Parmigiano-Reggiano cheese
1 pound shrimp, peeled
1 pound baby spinach, baby turnip greens,
    or arugula
Salt and freshly ground black pepper

Bring the milk and water to a simmer in a heavy-bottomed non-stick saucepan over medium heat. Add the grits and the garlic and bring just to a boil. Cook until soft and creamy, adding heavy cream as needed to make a loose, but not runny, mixture. Add as much butter and cheese as desired, stirring to make sure the cheese doesn't stick. Add the shrimp and cook a few minutes more until pink. Fold in the washed and dried greens and remove from the heat. The greens will cook in the hot grits. Serve in a chafing dish for a party or individually for an appetizer or main course.

Variation: Add enough cream to the grits to make them the consistency of a dip. Chop the shrimp and the greens before adding to the hot grits and serve with crisp tortilla chips.

Hot Grits Cakes with Tasso and Butterflied Shrimp

Serves 2 as an appetizer

The smaller a hot pepper, the hotter it is. Jalapeños are not the hottest of peppers, but they still have quite a zing. Be judicious about peppers, particularly if you are serving to guests, and add a little at a time, tasting all along.

A really good Parmesan is lost in this dish, so don't worry about not using the most expensive one. You could even use Romano. The combination of the seafood seasoning with the tasso dominates the flavor.

Salt
1 to 2 jalapeño peppers, seeded and chopped
2 cups cooked grits
2 tablespoons butter
1 cup chopped scallions

6 jumbo shrimp, peeled and butterflied
1/2 cup diced tasso or smoked ham
1 to 2 teaspoons seafood seasoning
1 cup heavy cream
1/2 cup grated Parmesan cheese

Butter an 8 x 8-inch baking dish. Add salt and jalapeños to the hot grits to taste. Spread the grits out in the baking dish. Refrigerate just long enough to harden.

Meanwhile, heat the butter in a sauté pan and add the scallions, shrimp, tasso, and seafood seasoning. Sauté until the shrimp fan outward, about 2 minutes. Remove the shrimp. Add the cream, bring to a boil, and reduce until slightly thickened. Add the Parmesan cheese and mix well. Add the shrimp and heat through.

Cut 2 large triangles out of the hardened grits and heat through in an oven or microwave. Spoon the shrimp mixture onto 2 plates. Sit the grits triangles on a slant atop the shrimp mixture and serve.

Grits Cakes

Grits cakes are a handy way to use leftover grits or to make grits ahead. They also have a "finished" look. I've seen them molded into hearts, pyramids, and many other shapes, as well as flattened into small round cakes. One way to shape them is to spread cooked grits on an oiled baking sheet. When cool, cut into shapes. Another way is to heap them in a loaf pan or other mold. When cool, turn out and slice or shape. A handy trick is to roll them two inches thick, wrap with plastic wrap, and roll again to shape like store-bought cookie dough. When ready to use, unwrap and slice. Cooked and cooled grits may be sautéed or grilled, or served as is as a platform for cold foods.

Shrimp Succotash on Deep-Fried Cheese Grits

Serves 8 as a starter or side dish

The taste of summer in this recipe will make it a favorite.

1 1/2 cups grated sharp cheddar cheese
2 tablespoons butter
3 cups cooked grits
2 slices bacon
1 red bell pepper, finely chopped
4 tablespoons finely chopped Vidalia
   or other sweet onion
1 1/2 cups cooked butter beans, butter peas,
   or baby limas
3 ears fresh corn, kernels cut off and cobs
   scraped for milk

2 pounds medium shrimp, peeled
1/4 cup heavy cream
1 egg beaten with 1 tablespoon water
panko*
Vegetable oil
Salt and freshly ground black pepper
1 teaspoon fresh chopped thyme
Hot sauce (optional)

Butter an 8 x 8-inch baking dish. Add the cheddar and butter to the hot grits. Spread the grits out in the baking dish. Cool to room temperature, cover, and refrigerate for up to 2 days.

Fry the bacon until crisp in a heavy-bottomed frying pan. Remove the bacon and drain on paper towels, leaving a small amount of the fat in the pan. Crumble the bacon and reserve. Add the red pepper and onion to the hot bacon fat, and cook, stirring, until they begin to soften. Add the butter beans, the corn and its milk, the shrimp, and the cream, stir to combine, and bring to a simmer. Cook for 3 minutes, or until shrimp turn pink.

Put the egg mixture and panko into separate shallow bowls. Cut the cold grits into eight squares. Fill a deep frying pan with oil approximately 3/4 inch deep, but no more than halfway up the sides. Heat the oil to 360 degrees F. Dip the squares into the egg, shaking off the excess, then into the panko. Fry them in the hot oil for approximately 2 minutes on each side, turning carefully, or until they are golden and hot through. Drain on paper towels. Salt and pepper the grits and succotash to taste.

Place the fried grits squares on 8 plates, spoon the succotash over them, sprinkle with the thyme, and serve.

*Available in the Asian foods section of most supermarkets.

⋅❧ Hush Hubbies ❧⋅

Serves 8 to 10

Delicious during Super Bowl games, or anytime you want a good nosh, my husband named them "hush hubbies." Add your own fresh chopped herbs to taste instead of the parsley.

The panko gives a distinctive crunch, but bread crumbs may be used if necessary.

1 pound medium shrimp, peeled
1/4 cup olive oil
1/4 cup dry sherry
Juice of 1 lemon
4 cups hot grits, cooked in 4 1/2 cups milk
1/3 cup mascarpone or cream cheese
½ cup butter, divided
3 tablespoons Worcestershire sauce

1/2 cup grated Parmigiano-Reggianno
1/3 cup finely chopped parsley
2 scallions, finely sliced, white and green separated, divided
3 egg yolks
Salt and freshly ground black pepper
2 cups panko*
1/2 cup vegetable oil, divided
Hot pepper jelly or chutney (optional)

Add the shrimp to the oil heated in a frying pan and sauté briefly until they turn pink. Do not overcook. Add the dry sherry and lemon juice together and toss the shrimp in the mixture. Set aside briefly, or refrigerate, covered, until needed.

Meanwhile, mix together the hot grits, mascarpone or cream cheese, 4 tablespoons of the butter, Worcestershire sauce, Parmigiano-Reggiano, parsley, all of the scallion whites, an equal amount of the scallion greens, and the egg yolks. Season to taste with salt and pepper. The mixture should be maleable. If too soggy, add a little of the panko. If too dry, add a little milk.

Drain the shrimp and pat with paper towels to dry slightly. Measure out enough of the grits mixture to thoroughly wrap each shrimp, leaving no pink showing through. Season the panko or bread crumbs with salt and pepper to taste. Gently roll each hush hubby in panko or bread crumbs.

Heat 2 tablespoons oil with 1 tablespoon butter until sizzling in a heavy-bottomed non-stick frying pan. Add 8 to 10 hush hubbies, taking care not to crowd the pan. Cook on the first side until brown, approximately 2 minutes or less, turn and finish browning on second side. Wipe the pan if necessary and repeat the process, adding oil and butter when necessary. Serve right away. Accompany with hot pepper jelly or chutney if a sauce is desired.

*Panko can be found in the Asian food section of most supermarkets.

Grits and Garlic Jalapeño Shrimp

This dish can be made in advance for quick cooking. Know your guests before adding all the chiles.

4 cups cooked grits
4 slices bacon
2 teaspoons ground cumin
1 teaspoon paprika
1/4 to 1 teaspoon cayenne pepper
Salt and freshly ground black pepper
1 pound medium shrimp, peeled

1 bunch scallions
1 to 2 red jalapeño chiles
1 to 2 green jalapeño chiles
2 tablespoons olive oil
4 garlic cloves, chopped
Juice of 2 limes

Spread the grits into a buttered 8 x 8-inch baking dish. Cool, cover, and refrigerate for up to 2 days.

Cut the cold grits into 4 equal squares. Fry the bacon in a heavy-bottomed frying pan until crisp. Remove the bacon and drain on paper towels, leaving the fat in the pan. Crumble the bacon and reserve. Heat the fat, add the 4 grits cakes, and cook quickly until golden on both sides. Remove the grits cakes and keep warm.

Combine the cumin, paprika, and the desired amount of cayenne pepper in a bowl. Add the shrimp and toss to coat evenly. Season to taste with salt and pepper.

Thinly slice the scallions on the diagonal. Stem and seed the jalapeños and slice evenly. Heat the olive oil in a sauté pan over medium-high heat. Add the shrimp and sauté until they turn pink, about 2 minutes. Add the scallions, jalapeños, garlic, and bacon and cook 1 minute longer. Remove from the heat and stir in the lime juice.

Place the grits cakes on 4 plates, spoon the shrimp and vegetables over top, and serve.

Green Onions vs. Scallions

Green onions are immature onions. When pulled from the ground they are not allowed to dry in the sun, and their greens are left attached. Their bulbs are round. Scallions have a flatter bulb, and will not grow into an onion. There is less volume to a scallion bulb, so substitute two to three scallions for one green onion bulb. The greens measure about the same.

Cold Shrimp Paste Spread

Makes 2 cups

This rich pink paste dates back in Georgia and South Carolina history. There are recipes for it in most coastal Southern cookbooks, like *Charleston Receipts* and *Two Hundred Years of Charleston Cooking*. It's smooth, buttery, and subtle, like a cold mousse or quenelle. Serve it on Grits Bread (see p. 124), Grits Cakes (see p. 27), or crackers.

1 1/2 cups butter, softened
1 1/2 pounds large shrimp, cooked and peeled
3/4 teaspoon salt
1/4 teaspoon fresh thyme

1/4 teaspoon freshly grated nutmeg
Dash cayenne pepper or hot sauce
Freshly ground black pepper
Chives for garnish

Line a loaf pan or other mold with plastic wrap. Whisk the butter until soft and white. Chop the shrimp very fine in a food processor or blender and add to the butter, combining well. Add the salt, thyme, nutmeg, and cayenne pepper or hot sauce and mix well. Season to taste with black pepper. Spread the shrimp paste in the loaf pan or mold. Cover and refrigerate until set. (Shrimp paste can be frozen. Defrost before serving.)

Hot or Cold Shrimp Paste

Makes 3 cups

This is the other of two famous shrimp pastes. Traditionally, it is served cold on toast points or with cold meats, but I like to serve it hot as a rich starter, like a quenelle, with Grits Bread (see p. 124), Grits Cakes (see p. 27), or crackers.

1 cup butter
1 pound large shrimp, cooked and peeled
Freshly grated nutmeg
Salt and freshly ground black pepper

Preheat an oven to 350 degrees F. Butter a loaf pan and line it with parchment paper or aluminum foil.

Whisk the butter until soft and white. Chop the shrimp finely in a food processor or blender and add to the butter, combining well. Season to taste with nutmeg, salt, and pepper. Put the shrimp paste in the loaf pan and bake for 30 minutes, or until the paste comes away from the sides of the pan and is light brown on top. Turn out of the pan by running a knife around the edge, or removing from the pan and peeling the paper off. Serve hot or cool to room temperature, cover, and refrigerate overnight. Slice and serve cold.

Grits Cakes and Roasted Red Pepper Sauce

Serves 8 as a starter

This is so pretty and easy . Both the grits cakes and the sauce may be made ahead and reheated.

4 cups cooked grits, cooked with
*   1 tablespoon chopped garlic*
¹/2 cup extra-sharp cheddar cheese
2 tablespoons chopped fresh chives
4 tablespoons butter, divided
Hot pepper sauce to taste
1 ¹/2 cups chicken stock
3 red bell peppers, seeded and chopped

3 to 4 tablespoons red wine vinegar, sherry wine
*   vinegar, or balsamic vinegar*
3 tablespoons sugar
Salt and freshly ground black pepper
1 log goat cheese, sliced into 8 pieces
1 pound medium peeled and cooked shrimp
16 chives

Butter a 9 x 5 x 2 ¹/2-inch loaf pan and line it with parchment paper or aluminum foil. Stir the hot grits, cheese, chives, and 2 tablespoons butter together. Season to taste with hot sauce. Pour the grits into the pan and refrigerate until chilled and firm.

Simmer the chicken stock and chopped peppers in a heavy-bottomed saucepan over medium heat for 10 minutes. Strain, reserving the liquid. Purée the peppers until smooth. Return them to the saucepan and add the vinegar, sugar, and reserved stock. Boil, stirring frequently, until thick and glossy. Season with salt and pepper to taste.

When ready to serve, unmold the grits and slice them into 8 grits cakes. Heat the remaining butter in a heavy-bottomed non-stick frying pan over medium-high heat. Cook the grits cakes for 5 minutes on each side, or until golden and heated through. Put 1 grits cake on each plate, spoon the pepper sauce over each, and top with a slice of goat cheese and several cooked shrimp. Garnish each with 2 chives and serve.

Spiced Shrimp Soup with Grits Cakes

This adaptation for tom yaam goong has far fewer chiles than the classic Thai soup. Ladling it over grits cakes changes the soup even more. Its up to you whether you want to add hot chiles to the soup or grits cakes. (Be sure to wear rubber gloves if you do.) I suggest that you try it first my way. I think you'll love it.

1 pound medium shrimp, preferably heads-on
6 stalks fresh lemongrass, outer leaves discarded
   and root ends trimmed
6 cups water
$^1/_4$ cup finely chopped well-washed coriander
   roots and/or stems*
2 quarter-sized pieces of fresh gingerroot,
   finely julienned

$^1/_4$ cup Asian fish sauce (nam pla)*
$^1/_4$ cup fresh lime juice
$^1/_2$ to 1 small fresh red or green Thai chili,* seeded and
   sliced very thin
Salt and freshly ground black pepper
Grits Cakes (see p. 27)
Fresh coriander leaves, thinly sliced kaffir lime leaves,*
   and small fresh red Thai chilies* for garnish if desired

Peel the shrimp, reserving the shell and heads. Cut 3 of the lemongrass stalks into 1-inch sections and crush lightly with the flat side of a heavy knife. Bring the crushed lemongrass, reserved shrimp shells and heads, water, and coriander roots to a boil. Reduce the heat and simmer, uncovered, for 20 minutes. Strain and discard the solids.

Thinly slice the lower 6 inches of the 3 remaining stalks of lemongrass, discarding the remainder of the stalks, and add to the strained broth along with the gingerroot. Simmer for 5 minutes. Add the shrimp and simmer for 2 minutes, or until the shrimp turn pink. Stir in the fish sauce, lime juice, and as much of the sliced chile as desired. Season with salt and pepper.

Serve with Grits Cakes, garnished with coriander leaves, lime leaves, and optional chilies.

*Available in the Asian foods section of most supermarkets.

Curried Thai Soup with Shrimp and Grits

Serves 4 to 6

Even the skeptical will make lip-smacking sounds after they eat this semi-Thai curry. Be judicious about the amount of curry paste you use, depending on the taste buds of those who will be eating. Usually served over rice, the grits give a wonderful change from ordinary Thai food, and will win your heart.

1 tablespoon vegetable oil
1 cup thinly sliced onion
1 cup chopped scallions
1 to 2 tablespoons Thai green curry paste*
1 (14-ounce) can unsweetened coconut milk*
1 cup chicken stock
3 tablespoons bottled Thai fish sauce (nam pla)*

2 teaspoons sugar
1 cup diced plum tomatoes
2 pounds large shrimp, peeled and deveined
4 cups cooked Lemon Grass Grits (see p. 114)
1 to 2 tablespoons chopped fresh basil and basil leaves
  or chopped fresh cilantro and cilantro leaves
Lime wedges

Heat the oil in a large heavy-bottomed frying pan. Add the onion and stir-fry until soft and beginning to brown, about 4 minutes. Reduce the heat to medium. Add the scallions and curry paste and stir until fragrant, about 1 minute. Add the coconut milk, chicken stock, fish sauce, and sugar and bring to a boil. Add the tomatoes and boil 2 minutes, stirring. Add the shrimp and cook, stirring often, for about 3 minutes, or until they turn pink.

Divide the hot grits between the bowls. Top with the soup. Garnish with basil or cilantro, and serve, passing the lime wedges separately.

Variations: Add snow peas and slivers of red or yellow bell pepper. Add chopped fresh Thai or other basil.

*Available in the Asian foods section of most supermarkets.

⊰ Glorious Seafood Stew ⊱

Serves 6

Stew is an inglorious name for delicious thick broth full of shrimp and scallops and studded with tomatoes and herbs. Saffron is expensive these days, but then so are scallops and shrimp—also worth the cost. This is a fabulous dish for favorite relatives or friends on a cold night.

1 to 2 teaspoons saffron, divided,
    soaked in 1/4 cup wine or stock, divided
4 cups cooked grits, cooked with water
    and shrimp stock
1/4 cup olive oil
1 1/2 large onions, cut in 1/2 inch pieces
3 garlic cloves, finely chopped
3/4 cup white wine
1 (1-pound-12-ounce) can peeled plum
    tomatoes, coarsely chopped

1 bay leaf
Salt and freshly ground black pepper
1 to 2 teaspoons sugar (optional)
1 1/2 tablespoons chopped fresh basil
2 1/2 tablespoons finely chopped fresh oregano or thyme
1 pound fresh shrimp, peeled
1 pound fresh sea scallops

Add half of the saffron mixture to the hot grits. Meanwhile, heat the oil in a large Dutch oven over medium heat. Add the onions and garlic and cook until soft, 5 to 7 minutes. Add the wine, the remaining saffron mixture, the tomatoes, and bay leaf and simmer, uncovered, until thickened, about 45 minutes. Season to taste with salt, pepper, and sugar (if using). Add the basil and oregano or thyme and continue cooking for a few minutes more to blend the flavors. (The stew may be made ahead to this point and refrigerated or frozen.)

When ready to serve, bring the stew to the boil. Add the shrimp and scallops, reduce the heat to a simmer, and cook 2 to 3 minutes, or until the shrimp turn pink and the scallops are opaque. Divide the grits between 6 bowls, top with the stew, garnish with herbs and serve.

This is not a gumbo in the strict sense, as it doesn't have a roux. I adapted it from a friend's recipe. It works as well with grits as with rice. You can use any type of sausage. Add the oysters and crabmeat or leave them out—your choice. It freezes well.

$^1/_3$ cup pork lard, chicken fat, or vegetable oil
10 cups sliced okra, (3 pounds) sliced
   $^1/_4$ inch thick, 2 cups reserved
2 cups chopped onions
1 cup chopped green bell pepper
2 cups chopped celery
10 cups Shrimp Stock (see p. 36), divided
3 cups fresh or canned chopped tomatoes,
   1 cup reserved
1 tablespoon white pepper
1 tablespoon cayenne pepper
2 teaspoons black pepper
6 garlic cloves, chopped
1 tablespoon chopped fresh oregano

$^1/_2$ cup unsalted butter
1 pound Andouille, kielbasa, or other smoked sausage,
   peeled and cut in $^1/_4$ inch slices
2 $^1/_2$ to 3 $^1/_2$ pounds medium shrimp, peeled
1 $^1/_2$ quarts shucked oysters
1 pound crabmeat
1 cup chopped scallion greens
Salt
1 to 2 tablespoons fresh lemon juice
1 to 2 tablespoons filé powder
16 cups cooked grits
Green hot sauce
Lemon wedges for garnish

Heat the fat in a very large heavy-bottomed pot. Add 6 cups okra and stir over medium-high heat for 10 to 15 minutes, or until the okra is browned. Add the onions, bell pepper, and celery, and cook for 5 minutes, stirring occasionally, to prevent scorching.

Add 2 cups shrimp stock and cook for 5 minutes, stirring and scraping often. Stir in 2 cups of the tomatoes and cook another 10 minutes, stirring and scraping as needed. Add another 4 cups stock and cook 5 minutes more. Stir in the white pepper, cayenne pepper, black pepper, garlic, and oregano. Add the rest of the stock, stirring well. Bring to a boil, add the sausage, return to a boil, reduce the heat, and simmer, covered, for 45 minutes, stirring occasionally. Add the reserved 2 cups okra and cook for 5 minutes. Add the shrimp, oysters, crabmeat, and scallion greens. Season with salt to taste and bring to a boil. Skim any fat from surface. Add the lemon juice to taste and the remaining okra and tomatoes. Add the filé powder to taste and sir to combine. Do not let the gumbo come back to a boil, but heat through.

Serve with the grits, green hot sauce, and lemon wedges.

Squash and Apple Soup with Shrimp and Grits Cakes

Serves 6 to 8

My assistant, Mary Ellen Battistelli, wrote the recipe for this soup. It can be made in about 30 minutes. It uses everything at its peak. But if you wait until the end of summer, just when the shrimp in Georgia and South Carolina are coming in, it is even better. There is a variance in liquid as liquid may be lost in the cooking.

4 to 6 cups shrimp or chicken stock
4 ears fresh corn
2 tablespoons butter or olive oil
1 medium onion, chopped
1 Fuji apple, chopped
$1/8$ to $1/4$ teaspoon curry powder
1 cup cored, peeled, seeded, and
   chopped tomatoes
2 small or 1 medium zucchini, (about $1/2$ pound)
   chopped roughly

1 clove garlic, chopped
Salt and freshly ground black pepper
1 pound peeled shrimp
$1/2$ cup chopped fresh basil leaves
1 teaspoon balsamic or other flavorful vinegar,
   or to taste
12 to 14 Grits Cakes (see p. 20), cut in triangles

Heat the stock in a large, heavy-bottomed deep pot. Cut the kernels from the corn cobs, scrape the cobs for their milk, and add the cobs and corn milk to the stock, setting the corn kernels aside until later. Simmering the cobs in the stock will add flavor.

Heat the butter or oil in a separate large deep saucepan. Add the onion and cook, stirring, until it begins to soften, about 5 minutes. Add the apple and the curry powder and cook a few minutes more. Stir frequently. Add the tomatoes, zucchini, and garlic, and season to taste with salt and pepper. Cook, stirring occasionally, for 10 minutes.

Remove the corncobs from the stock and add the stock to the vegetables. Bring back to a boil, lower the heat, and cook until the zucchini is tender but not mushy, about 5 minutes. Add more stock if necessary. Add the shrimp, corn kernels, and most of the basil. Add the vinegar. Taste and adjust the seasoning as necessary. Cook for 2 minutes, or until the shrimp turn pink. Serve with the Grits Cakes and garnish with the remaining basil.

Indian-Style Chicken, Shrimp and Grits Stew

Serves 6 to 8

This make-ahead, hearty, well-flavored recipe is a good company recipe as well as a good family recipe. It is very tasty and can easily be doubled if desired. Cutting up a whole chicken guarantees even-sized pieces for cooking. Store-bought pre-packaged chicken parts are frequently larger and take longer to cook.

1/2 cup plus 1 teaspoon extra-virgin
olive oil, divided
4 cups cooked Lemon Grass Grits (see p. 114)
1/2 cup fresh lime juice, divided
3 garlic cloves, chopped, divided
Salt and freshly ground black pepper
1 (3- to 4-pound) chicken, cut into 8 pieces
1 pound medium shrimp, peeled

2 medium onions, chopped
1 red or yellow bell pepper, seeded and chopped
1 pound fresh tomatoes, chopped
3 to 4 cups chicken stock
1 to 2 small hot peppers, seeded and chopped or red
pepper paste to taste
1 cup well-stirred canned unsweetened coconut milk
1/2 cup chopped fresh cilantro

Stir 1 teaspoon of the olive oil into the hot grits.

Mix together 1/4 cup olive oil, 1/4 cup lime juice, half the garlic, 1 teaspoon salt, and 1/4 teaspoon pepper in a large plastic bag. Add the chicken and mix to coat. Marinate in the refrigerator for at least 30 minutes, or overnight.

Mix together 2 tablespoons olive oil, 2 tablespoons lime juice, the remaining garlic, and 1/4 teaspoon pepper in another plastic bag. Add the shrimp and mix to coat. Marinate in the refrigerator for at least 30 minutes but not more than 1 hour.

Remove the chicken from the marinade and pat dry. Heat the remaining oil in a large heavy-bottomed pot and heat over medium-high heat until hot but not smoking. Add the chicken to the pot skin-side down, starting with the larger pieces and the dark meat. Do not crowd the pot. When brown, turn, brown the other side, and remove. Repeat with remaining chicken. Add the onions and bell pepper to the pot and cook, stirring occasionally and scraping the bottom of the pan until the onions are golden brown, 6 to 8 minutes. Add the tomatoes and stir a few minutes over the heat until their juice is rendered. Stir in 2 cups chicken stock and hot peppers and bring to a simmer. Add the chicken, along with juices accumulated on the plate, and simmer, covered, until the chicken is cooked through, 25 to 30 minutes, adding more stock if necessary.

Remove the chicken, let it cool enough to remove the meat from the bones and skin, and tear it into edible-sized pieces. Skim any fat off of the top of the stew. (Both the chicken and the stew may be made ahead and refrigerated for a day or two.)

When ready to serve, bring the stew to the boil. Reduce heat and stir in the chicken and shrimp and cook until the chicken is heated through and the shrimp turn pink, 3 to 4 minutes. Add the coconut milk, the remaining lime juice, and half the cilantro. Season to taste with salt, pepper, and more of the hot peppers, if desired. Serve over the grits. Garnish with the remaining cilantro.

Making Shrimp Stock, Lemon Grass Stock and Saffron Stock

Just as chicken stock can be made from the broth when poaching chicken, the broth that shrimp are poached in can be made into a flavorful shrimp stock. It can be enriched if, after peeling the shrimp, the shells are returned to the pot of broth and allowed to simmer in the broth a little longer. If heading and shelling the shrimp before cooking them, use the heads and shells to make a nice stock from scratch.

If cooking a pound or so of shrimp at a time, save their shells in a bag in the freezer until there is enough to make a pot of stock. The same applications apply to the heads if heading and shelling. As with other stocks, shrimp stock can be reduced down to produce a stronger flavor, though it will never congeal as animal stocks do. Reducing the quantity of the liquid also makes it handier for freezing in small containers, to be used later for the enrichment of a dish or for adding back liquid to return it to a stock.

Other flavorings may be added to the stock, such as carrot or onion pieces, peppercorns, parsley or other herb stalks, tomato peels, lemon, lime or orange peel, lemon grass, ginger, coriander seed, and saffron, to name a few. Grits cooked in shrimp stock require very little else in the way of seasonings, as the stock adds a real dimension to the grits.

Lemon Grass Stock to Make Lemon Grass Grits

I first saw lemon grass stock in Australia, where the chef was using it to flavor rice. Now I grow lemon grass myself and use it for grits. Add several lemon grass stalks, several slices of ginger the size of a quarter, some kafir lime leaves, coriander root, stem, or leaves to a shrimp or chicken stock and cook as long as possible to extract flavor. Strain and boil down to reduce to the amount of liquid needed for the grits. If there is still not sufficient seasoning, add a small amount of chopped lemon grass and fresh ginger to the grits and stock while cooking the grits. (Kafir lime, coriander, and ginger also grow well in the Carolina lowcountry and may be added to stock.)

Saffron Stock to Make Saffron Grits

Slake several strands of saffron in lemon juice or water to bring out the flavor, then add to stock and simmer with the stock until the flavor permeates. If the flavor is not strong enough, do the same with several more strands of saffron in the liquid you are using for the grits. Saffron varies considerably in flavor from country to country, and how long you have had it.

Anytime Shrimp & Grits

Acadian Peppered Shrimp and Grits

Terry Thompson, a former student of mine now turned big-time chef and cookbook author, gave me this recipe when I was writing *New Southern Cooking*. She has a special taste for the piquant since she is from Louisiana. You will always find a bottle of hot sauce in her pocket when she's cooking.

2 cups butter
1/2 cup fresh lemon juice
2 teaspoons chopped fresh basil
1 to 2 teaspoons cayenne pepper
2 teaspoons chopped fresh oregano or marjoram
5 cloves garlic, minced

1 bay leaf, crumbled
1/2 cup finely ground black pepper
4 pounds large shrimp in shells
Salt
2 cups cooked grits, cooked with shrimp stock or water
Hot crusty bread

Heat the butter in a large, deep-sided frying pan over low heat. Raise the heat to medium and add all of the ingredients except the shrimp, salt, grits and bread. Cook, stirring often, until browned to a rich mahogany color, about 10 minutes. Add the shrimp, stirring and turning to coat well with the seasoned butter. Cook until the shrimp have turned a rich deep pink, about 10 minutes. Season to taste with salt. Serve the hot grits in bowls and the shrimp in their shells, peeling them at the table. Accompany with hot bread to dip in the sauce.

Folly Island Shrimp and Grits

Makes 4 cakes as an appetizer

Folly Island is located about 15 minutes from downtown Charleston, South Carolina. This recipe was found online, but it was so unusual, made with cream cheese and lime juice, that I tried it and loved it. And it is quick, quick, quick, especially if you use quick grits.

4 tablespoons butter, divided
3 tablespoons cream cheese
2 tablespoons half-and-half
1/3 cup chopped scallions

2 cups cooked grits, cooked with chicken stock
Salt and freshly ground black pepper
1 pound medium shrimp, peeled
2 tablespoons fresh lime juice

Stir 1 tablespoon of the butter, the cream cheese, half-and-half, and half the scallions into the hot grits. Season to taste with salt and pepper.

Heat the remaining butter in a heavy-bottomed frying pan, add the shrimp, and cook for 2 minutes, or until they turn pink. Add the lime juice. Divide the grits between two plates, top with the shrimp, spoon on the pan juices, garnish with the remaining scallions, and serve.

Benne Seed and Orange Juice Shrimp and Grits

Makes 4 servings

Benne, the African word for sesame seed, combines with orange juice to give an extraordinary flavor and texture to this spicy marinated shrimp. The sauce permeates the grits.

2 cups fresh orange juice, divided
2 tablespoons ground cumin
2 medium onions, coarsely chopped
1 tablespoon coarsely ground black pepper
1 teaspoon red pepper flakes
1 teaspoon salt
1 teaspoon Worcestershire sauce

2 teaspoons chopped or grated fresh ginger
1 tablespoon chopped fresh thyme
2 1/2 pounds medium shrimp, peeled
Zest of 3 oranges
4 cups cooked grits
1/2 cup sesame seeds, back and/or white

Mix 1 cup orange juice, cumin, onions, pepper, red pepper flakes, salt, Worcestershire, ginger, and half the thyme in a mixing bowl or large plastic bag. Add the shrimp and marinate for 1 hour in the refrigerator, turning 2 to 3 times.

Preheat the broiler. Remove the shrimp from the marinade and place them on an aluminum foil-covered broiler pan. Broil for 2 minutes, turn, and broil quickly on the other side. Remove from the oven. Meanwhile, heat the marinade with the orange zest and the remaining orange juice.

Arrange the hot grits on the bottom of a serving dish, top with the shrimp, spoon on the sauce, sprinkle with the sesame seeds, and reserved thyme and serve family-style.

Polly Kosko's Citrus and Butter Shrimp over Lemon Grass Grits

Serves 6 to 8

Polly Kosko is the long-time Public Relations Director of South Carolina Educational Television and a real mover and shaker. Her dad is famous for this dish. He prefers to use garlic powder. It's really a take-however-many-you-caught amount of shrimp recipe, and it is absolutely delicious. If you don't like the idea of peeling the shrimp at the table and eating the grits with the juices, then peel the shrimp and cook them a little less time, checking carefully to be sure they don't overcook.

1 cup butter, room temperature, divided
3 garlic cloves, chopped
2 pounds medium or large shrimp, shells on
2 Valencia oranges, sliced thinly

2 lemons, sliced thinly
4 cups cooked Lemon Grass Grits (see p. 114)
Crusty bread

Preheat an oven to 350 degrees F.

Butter an 8 ½ x 11-inch baking dish. Beat half the butter with the garlic. Put a layer of shrimp on the bottom of the baking dish. Add a layer of orange and lemon slices and dot with some of the garlic butter. Add more shrimp and cover with orange and lemon slices and dot with more butter. Continue until all the shrimp are used, finishing with orange and lemon slices, and garlic butter. Add more butter if desired. Cover with aluminum foil. Bake for 30 minutes, remove the foil, stir, and continue baking until the shrimp are pink. Serve with hot Lemon Grass Grits and crusty bread to mop up the sauce.

Herbed-Cheese Grits, Shrimp and Collards Casserole

This doubles easily, and is a wonderful dish to make when the weather is nippy. You may use turnip greens if you prefer.

*4 cups cooked quick grits, cooked
   with chicken stock*
*1 cup garlic-herb cheese, such as Boursin,
   or herbed goat cheese*
1 pound cooked shrimp

*1/3 cup sliced sun-dried tomatoes
   packed in oil, drained*
2 tablespoons chopped fresh basil
*1 cup washed, stemmed, chopped or sliced
   collards, lightly steamed*

Preheat an oven to 350 degrees F.

Mix together the grits and cheese until the cheese melts. Add the shrimp, sun-dried tomatoes, basil, and collard greens and spread the mixture out in a 10-inch buttered casserole dish. Bake until heated through, about 20 minutes, and serve.

New Orleans-Style Grits Cakes with Shrimp and Tasso

It is hard to know how long cooks in New Orleans have been making shrimp and grits, but now the dish is as familiar there as it is along the East Coast. Tasso, pork that has been cured, highly seasoned, and then smoked, is frequently an addition. Although it is frequently called tasso ham, it is actually made from the shoulder. The Louisiana and Mississippi affection for tasso and peppers doesn't always mesh with every palette, so this recipe leaves a lot of leeway for your taste buds. A top-quality Parmesan is not needed for these recipes as the tasso, peppers and Old Bay are so dominant.

2 cups cooked grits, cooked with water and $^1/_2$
    to 1 seeded and chopped jalapeño, as desired
2 tablespoons butter
1 cup chopped scallions
6 jumbo shrimp, peeled and butterflied

$^1/_2$ cup diced tasso
2 teaspoons Old Bay seasoning
1 cup heavy cream
$^1/_2$ cup fresh grated Parmesan cheese

Pour the grits into a buttered 8 x 8-inch baking dish and refrigerate to harden. Cut the grits into 4 triangles, or any other shape you wish. When ready to serve, heat through in an oven or a microwave.

Heat the butter in a heavy-bottomed frying pan. Add the scallions, shrimp, tasso, and Old Bay seasoning. Cook quickly over high heat for about 2 minutes, or until the shrimp turn pink. Add the cream and Parmesan cheese and boil for 30 seconds to reduce. Place the grits cakes on two plates, top with the shrimp and tasso sauce, and serve.

Corny Grits, Shallots, and Shrimp

This party all-in-one dish just about makes a full meal. Only a salad or green vegetable is needed. Fresh corn makes it all the better, but since corn freezes so well, feel free to use it in the winter. Everything but the shrimp is together; the shrimp are served separately.

4 cups cooked grits
1 to 2 tablespoons olive oil, divided
1 cup chopped shallots
1 teaspoon chopped fresh thyme leaves or
   1/3 teaspoon dried thyme
2 cups frozen yellow corn kernels, thawed
   and divided

3/4 cup chopped scallion greens, to taste
1/2 cup water
Hot sauce
Salt
3 tablespoons butter
2 pounds shrimp, peeled

Stir the cooked grits with a little of the oil. Heat enough of the remaining oil to cover the bottom of a heavy frying pan. Add the shallots and sauté until lightly golden, about 5 minutes. Add the thyme and 1 1/2 cups corn. Sauté for 3 minutes. Remove the pan from the heat. Meanwhile, purée the remaining corn, scallion greens and the water in a food processor. Add the shallot and corn mixture, purée, then stir all into the grits. Season to taste with hot sauce and salt. Heat the butter in the frying pan, add the shrimp, and sauté until the shrimp turn pink. Serve the shrimp and grits separately, or mound the grits on a platter and surround them with the shrimp.

Shrimp Grits Cakes with Lemon Sour Cream Sauce

When you compare the price difference in crab cakes and shrimp cakes, and you taste these, you will think, why should I bother with crab? These are not too bready and have a very moist interior with a crisp exterior— just as shrimp or crab cakes should have. These grits are exceptional if cooked in shrimp stock.

1 cup cooked grits
6 tablespoons butter, divided
1/4 cup finely chopped red onion
3 scallions, finely chopped, white only
3 tablespoons finely chopped red bell pepper
Seasoning spices (optional)
1 pound shrimp, peeled
1 tablespoon white wine
4 tablespoons lemon juice, divided

1 1/4 cups panko or bread crumbs, divided
1/8 teaspoon cayenne pepper
1/2 cup freshly grated Parmesan cheese
Salt and freshly ground black pepper
2 eggs, beaten
1 to 2 tablespoons vegetable oil
1/2 cup mayonnaise
1/2 cup sour cream
Fresh dill or fennel fronds to garnish

Stir the grits with 2 tablespoons butter. Heat 3 tablespoons butter in a large heavy-bottomed frying pan. Add the onion, scallions, and bell pepper. Cook until soft, about 5 minutes. Add seasoning spices, if desired.

Remove the vegetables with a slotted spoon and set aside. Add the shrimp, wine and 2 tablespoons lemon juice to the pan. Cook until the shrimp are just pink. Remove with a slotted spoon and coarsely chop. Put the vegetables and shrimp back in the pan, along with 1/4 cup panko or bread crumbs, the grits, cayenne pepper and Parmesan. Season to taste with salt and pepper. Slowly add enough eggs to allow the mixture to stick together. When sufficient eggs are added, fry a small amount, taste and check texture. If it breaks apart while frying or is too dry, adjust with mayonnaise or more panko or seasoning. Drop 1/4 cup of the mixture on a non-stick baking sheet and flatten into a cake, using a spatula. Repeat using all of the mixture. Cover and chill for at least 2 hours, or overnight.

Coat the shrimp cakes with the remaining panko. Heat the oil and remaining butter in a non-stick frying pan. When sizzling, add the shrimp cakes, making sure they do not touch. Cook on one side until golden brown, turn and cook the other side. Remove with a slotted spatula and drain on paper towels before removing to platter or individual plates.

Stir together the mayonnaise, sour cream, and remaining lemon juice to make the sauce. Serve on lettuce or arugula. Garnish with the dill or fennel fronds.

Marion Sullivan's Shrimp and Grits

Co-author Marion Sullivan's version of the Lowcountry favorite owes its inspiration to Chapel Hill, North Carolina. She created it after eating Bill Neal's Shrimp and Grits at his restaurant there. She owes the grits to a fine South Carolina chef, her good friend Philip Bardin. No one has ever beaten them.

1 1/2 cups chicken stock
1 1/2 cups milk
3/4 cup yellow stone-ground grits
3/4 cup heavy cream
6 tablespoons unsalted butter, divided
8 strips bacon, cut in slices
1 cup chopped yellow onion
4 large cloves garlic, chopped

1/2 pound cremini mushrooms, cleaned and sliced
3 cups diced summer tomatoes or 1 (14 1/2-ounce) can tomato wedges, drained and diced
2 teaspoons Worcestershire sauce
Dash of Tabasco
1 pound medium shrimp, peeled
Salt and freshly ground black pepper

Bring the chicken stock and milk to a boil in a heavy-bottomed saucepan. Stir in the grits and simmer over medium heat, stirring frequently, until they begin to thicken and soften, about 30 minutes. You may need to add more milk as you go. Stir in the cream and 4 tablespoons butter and continue to simmer until the grits are soft and creamy. Stir frequently because milk solids burn easily.

Sauté the bacon until crisp. Remove from the pan and reserve. Add remaining butter to the pan and heat with the bacon fat. Add the onion and garlic and sauté until they begin to soften, about 3 minutes. Add the mushrooms and sauté until they begin to soften, about 3 minutes. Add the tomatoes, Worcestershire, and Tabasco. Simmer for 20 minutes to blend the flavors. Add the shrimp and sauté, stirring, until they turn pink. Season to taste with salt and pepper.

Divide the hot grits between four plates, spoon on the shrimp and sauce, and serve.

Sausage, Shrimp, Apple and Fennel Grits Strata

Serves 4

The best thing to do when making a grits casserole is to make two. An extra grits casserole in the freezer means you can serve it as is for an emergency or use it as a basis for this strata. Fennel may be sold as anise in some markets.

1 recipe cheese grits casserole or jalapeño grits casserole, without the shrimp (see p. 116), divided
1/2 pound chicken sausage, preferably sweet Italian
4 tablespoons butter, divided
1 onion, finely chopped
1 bulb fennel, cored and chopped, fronds reserved

2 Granny Smith apples, peeled if desired
1 pound small or medium shrimp, peeled
8 eggs
2 cups milk
2 cups grated white cheddar cheese, divided
3 tablespoons fresh thyme, basil, oregano, or marjoram (optional)
Salt and freshly ground black pepper

Preheat an oven to 325 degrees F.

Cut the grits casserole into 3 pieces that you will use to make 3 layers in a deep 8 x 8-inch buttered baking dish, and put 1 layer in the bottom. Prick the sausage. Heat 2 tablespoons butter in a large non-stick frying pan and sauté the sausage, onion, and fennel until the sausage is light brown and onion and fennel are soft. Remove and set aside. Core and slice the apples into wedges and add to the frying pan with the remaining butter. Sauté over medium-high heat until the apples are cooked even and slightly brown at the edges. Add the shrimp and sauté briefly. Remove the pan from heat and set aside.

Whisk the eggs just enough to mix. Whisk in the milk and half of the cheese. Add the sausage, onion, and fennel to the shrimp in the frying pan. Add the herbs, if desired. Season to taste with salt and pepper. Top the bottom layer of the grits casserole with half the shrimp mixture and one-third of the remaining cheese. Top with the second layer of the grits casserole. Add the last of the shrimp mixture and the second third of the cheese. Top with the remaining grits casserole piece. Pour the milk and egg mixture over the casserole. Sprinkle the top of the casserole with the remaining cheese. Bake for 45 minutes to 1 hour, or until a knife comes out clean.

Madeira-Glazed Shrimp with Parmesan Grits and Red-Eye Gravy

Serves 4

Madeira is famous in the South as the wine of choice for George Washington, who reputedly drank a pint of this fortified wine a day. The combination of the sweetness of the Coca-Cola and the richness of the Madeira bring a completely different touch to the dish. Red-eye gravy was traditionally made with country ham that had a round bone in the center, hence the "red eye." Coca-Cola, coffee, or water would be added at the end to soften the ham and provide a gravy.

3 tablespoons butter, divided
2 cups cooked grits, cooked with milk
Salt and freshly ground black pepper
4 ounces country ham, diced
1 1/2 cups stemmed and sliced shiitake mushrooms
1 cup finely chopped red or yellow bell pepper
1/2 cup chopped onion
2 teaspoons chopped fresh thyme

1 cup chicken stock
1/2 cup Coca-Cola, coffee, or water
1/2 cup seeded chopped tomatoes
1/4 cup Madeira
2 teaspoons cornstarch
1 teaspoon hot pepper sauce, optional
1 pound large uncooked shrimp, peeled
Freshly grated Parmesan cheese

Add 1 tablespoon of the butter to the grits and season to taste with salt and pepper.

Melt the remaining butter in large heavy-bottomed frying pan over medium-high heat. Add the ham and sauté until brown, about 2 minutes. Add the mushrooms, peppers, onion, and thyme and sauté for 3 minutes. Add the stock, Coca-Cola, and tomatoes. Bring to a boil, and boil until the liquid is reduced by half. Mix the Madeira and cornstarch in a small bowl. Add to the sauce and bring to a boil, stirring constantly. Reduce the heat and simmer until thickened, about 3 minutes. Add the hot pepper sauce, if desired. Season to taste with salt and pepper. (Can be made in advance to this point, refrigerated and reheated before using.) Add the shrimp and cook until the shrimp turn pink, about 3 minutes.

Divide the grits between four plates. Spoon the shrimp and gravy over them, sprinkle with Parmesan cheese, and serve.

How Do You Like Your Grits?

Grits are as personal as biscuits. Some prefer their grits thick. Others want them sauce-like. Some use a spoon to eat grits; others a fork. The late Strom Thurmond, the legendary U.S. Senator from South Carolina, would have his grits topped with sunny-side-up eggs. He'd crisscross with a knife and fork until all were blended. Once mingled, he would gulp them down in large mouthfuls, interspersed with downing whole glasses of prune juice, warm water and skim milk, and bites of buttered whole wheat toast. Within minutes, he was back to shaking hands and greeting potential voters.

Those who like cheese added to their grits range from those who add the little tube of so-called garlic cheese to goat cheese or fresh grated Parmigiano-Reggiano, the king of cheeses. I have hollowed out a half-wheel of this cheese and poured in parmesan-laden grits cooked first with cream and butter and topped with sautéed shrimp slathered in butter and garlic.

It is endless, this recitation of what can be done with shrimp and grits. You will find your own version of shrimp and grits, and defend it from all encroachments, and it will become "your recipe."

Okra, Shrimp and Grits in a Tangy Garlic Butter Sauce

This recipe was created for some German guests who called at the last moment when their plane was delayed at the airport. It was an unusually warm day, and it shocked them that we could eat outdoors in February. The mixture was poured over the grits and the guests peeled their own shrimp. (Of course, the shrimp may be peeled in advance.) Be sure to have plenty of napkins if your guests have to peel their own.

4 cups cooked grits, cooked with water and
   half-and-half
1 cup plus 3 tablespoons butter, divided
1 1/4 pounds okra, tipped and tailed
3 large garlic cloves, chopped
4 shallots, chopped

1 teaspoon cayenne pepper
1/2 to 1 tablespoon chopped fresh marjoram
1/2 to 1 tablespoon chopped fresh rosemary
2 pounds large shrimp, unpeeled
Salt and freshly ground black pepper

Stir the grits with 3 tablespoons butter. Bring a pot of water to a boil, add the okra, and boil for 2 minutes. Drain and refresh under cold water. Drain and set aside.

Heat the remaining butter in a large heavy-bottomed frying pan. Add the garlic, shallots, cayenne pepper, marjoram, and rosemary and cook over medium heat for 3 minutes without browning. Add the shrimp and cook until they start to turn pink on one side, about 2 minutes. Turn. Add the drained okra and cook until the shrimp are pink on both sides and the okra is reheated, about 3 minutes. Season to taste with salt and pepper and serve over the hot grits.

Short Cook

Bacon, Shrimp and Grits Frittata

Serves 2

A frittata is a flat version of an omelet, and like an omelet, the contents can be varied with what is at hand. Easily adapted for a fun brunch or an intimate Sunday supper, it is simple to cook and adaptable, and a fabulous use for leftover grits, bacon, shrimp and other of the ingredients. For a thicker frittata, use a smaller pan, remembering that it will take longer to cook.

3/4 cup cooked grits
2 tablespoons olive oil
1 1/2 cups finely chopped red or yellow bell pepper
2 to 3 strips bacon, cut into slices and cooked
  until crisp, or 1 slice smoked sausage,
  chopped into 1/2-inch pieces
1/4 pound medium shrimp, peeled

4 large eggs, lightly beaten
2 to 3 scallions, white and green parts, sliced
1/2 cup finely grated sharp cheddar cheese
1/4 cup Parmesan cheese, preferably Parmigiano-Reggiano
Cayenne pepper
Salt

Spread the hot grits 1/2-inch thick on a non-stick baking sheet. Chill for at least 30 minutes. When ready to use, cut in 1/2-inch pieces.

Preheat the broiler. Heat 1 tablespoon olive oil in a 9-inch non-stick frying pan. Add the bell pepper and sauté briefly with the bacon or sausage and shrimp until the shrimp turn pink. Whisk the eggs with the scallions, cheddar, and Parmesan in a bowl. Add cayenne pepper and salt to taste. Stir in the bell pepper mixture and the pieces of grits.

Wipe out the pan if necessary. Add the remaining oil to the same frying pan and, when very hot, but not smoking, pour in the egg mixture and cook the frittata over medium heat, without stirring, for about 8 to 10 minutes. The center should be a little soft, and the edges will be set. Wrap the handle in a double thickness of aluminum foil and broil the frittata for a few minutes until golden on top. Let the frittata set in the pan a few minutes. Slide onto a serving plate and cut into wedges to serve.

Short-Cook Shrimp and Grits

This is a version of a timeless recipe that is loosely known as "Shrimp Scampi." But it truly is quick—less than 10 minutes, particularly if you have been clever enough to freeze some grits ahead of time. The recipe doubles easily to serve four.

2 cups cooked grits, cooked with shrimp stock,
  milk, or water
Salt and freshly ground black pepper
4 tablespoons butter
1/4 cup olive oil

2 garlic cloves, crushed with salt
2 tablespoons chopped fresh parsley
Dash of cayenne pepper
Juice of 1 lemon
1/2 pound medium shrimp, peeled

Preheat the broiler.

Season the hot grits to taste with salt and pepper. Heat the butter, oil, and garlic in a broiler-proof frying pan. Stir in the parsley, cayenne pepper, and lemon juice. Add the shrimp, tossing to coat. Place the pan in the oven and broil 6 inches from the heat, 3 to 5 minutes, turning halfway through cooking, until the shrimp turn pink. (Alternately, sauté the shrimp over medium heat for 3 minutes, or until they turn pink.)

Divide the grits between two plates, put the shrimp on top of them, spoon on the juices, and serve.

This combo satisfies that yearning for something familiar for a fast lunch. It may be the all-time comfort food. Vary it by making hot Grits Cakes (see p. 27) and using two as sandwiches for the B, L, and T. Although the package directions say that quick grits can be cooked in as little as 5 minutes, a creamier consistency may be had by cooking them longer. Cover the pan to prevent unnecessary evaporation of the liquid.

4 tablespoons butter
4 cups cooked grits, cooked with water and
 half-and-half
4 strips bacon, cut into ¹/4 inch slices
1 pound small shrimp, peeled
3 cloves garlic, minced

4 thinly sliced scallions, white and green parts separated
¹/4 cup flour
2 medium tomatoes, seeded and diced
1 ¹/2 cups half-and-half or milk
Salt and freshly ground black pepper
6 large leaves arugula, washed

Add the butter to the hot grits. Cook the bacon in a heavy-bottomed frying pan until crisp, 5 to 10 minutes, stirring as needed. Remove and drain on paper towels. Add the shrimp, garlic, and the white parts of the scallions to the bacon grease. Cook, stirring occasionally, until the shrimp turn pink. Remove the shrimp with a slotted spoon and set aside.

Sprinkle the flour into the pan and stir until well blended. Add the tomatoes and half-and-half and stir until well blended. Cook, stirring occasionally, until the gravy thickens slightly. Season to taste with salt and pepper. Divide the grits between four plates. Spoon the gravy over the grits and sprinkle the shrimp, bacon, and green parts of the scallions over the top. Garnish with the arugula and serve.

For additional serving ideas with this same recipe, try making a sandwich (see the facing page) or hors d'oeuvres (right).

Mediterranean Grits with Shrimp and Roasted Red Bell Peppers

Serves 4

In this unusual recipe, the grits are cooked with garlic, shallots, and thyme and have a Mediterranean flavor. There are many varieties of roasted red peppers for sale. They are handy to keep on the shelf to quickly enhance a quick dish.

2 red bell peppers
2 tablespoons butter
3 garlic cloves, chopped
2 shallots, chopped
1 1/2 teaspoons chopped fresh thyme
1 cup quick grits
3 1/2 cups chicken stock

3 tablespoons heavy cream
1 teaspoon hot pepper sauce
1 teaspoon salt
1/4 teaspoon freshly ground black pepper
1 1/2 pounds large shrimp, peeled
1 cup crumbled feta cheese
Chopped fresh thyme or oregano

Preheat an oven to 400 degrees F. Butter an 11 x 7-inch glass baking dish.

Char the peppers over a gas flame or in the broiler until blackened on all sides. Put them in a plastic bag and let them stand for 10 minutes. Peel, seed, and coarsely chop the peppers.

Melt the butter in large heavy-bottomed saucepan over medium heat. Add the garlic, shallots, and thyme and sauté until the shallots soften, about 2 minutes. Add the grits and stir for 1 minute. Whisk in the stock and cream. Simmer, stirring occasionally, until the liquid is absorbed and the grits are thick and tender, about 8 minutes. Whisk in the hot pepper sauce, salt, and pepper. Fold in the roasted bell peppers. Spread the grits in the baking dish. (This can be made 2 hours ahead. Let stand at room temperature.)

Laying them on their sides, press the shrimp on top of the grits. Sprinkle with the cheese. Bake until the grits are heated through, the shrimp turn pink, and the cheese begins to brown, about 20 minutes. Garnish with the thyme or oregano and serve.

Southern Cheese Grits with Tomato Conserve and Shrimp

Serves 4

Tomato conserves vary considerably in the South, but they all are a tad sweet with a bit of dash from the cider vinegar, and more like a catsup than a marinara sauce. They bring this sweet-sour taste to the shrimp and cheese-laden grits. The bacon is just enough meat and just enough crunch to bring the dish up to total fulfillment and comfort.

4 tablespoons butter, divided
1 cup grated cheddar cheese
4 cups cooked grits, cooked with milk
2 pounds shrimp, peeled
1/2 pound bacon, cooked crisp and crumbled
1 medium onion, chopped

2 tablespoons chopped garlic
1 (28-ounce) can diced tomatoes
1 (28-ounce) can crushed tomatoes
1/4 cup cider vinegar
1/3 cup brown sugar

Add 2 tablespoons butter and cheese to the hot grits. Heat the remaining butter in a large heavy-bottomed frying pan and sauté the peeled shrimp quickly until they turn pink. Remove the shrimp with a slotted spoon and set aside. To make the conserve, add the onion and garlic to the butter and cook until soft, about 4 minutes. Add the tomatoes, vinegar, and brown sugar and simmer for 15 to 20 minutes, or until the sauce is thick and jam-like. Stir in the shrimp and serve over the hot grits. Top with the crumbled bacon.

Quick Tomato-Bacon Shrimp and Grits

It's not necessary to be exact about this recipe, which makes it a good one to remember when time is of the essence. The shrimp and grits deliver flavor as well as texture. The bacon garnish adds crunch, and the whole dish, including the scallions, is pretty enough to serve to company. If scallions are not available, garnish with chives.

2 cups cooked grits, cooked in shrimp stock
   or water
2 tablespoons butter
6 strips bacon, cut in $^1/4$ inch slices
1 pound small shrimp, peeled
2 garlic cloves, chopped
3 thinly sliced scallions, white and green
   parts separated

$^1/4$ cup flour
2 medium tomatoes, peeled, seeded, and sliced
   into strips
1 $^1/2$ cups half-and-half or milk
Salt
Cayenne pepper or white pepper
Arugula, for garnish (optional)

Stir the hot grits and butter to combine. Sauté the bacon until crisp. Remove one-third of the bacon, drain, and set aside as a garnish. Add the shrimp, garlic, and scallion whites to the remaining bacon and grease. Sauté until the shrimp turn pink, about 3 minutes. Remove the shrimp. Sprinkle in the flour and stir until incorporated. Add the tomatoes and half-and-half, stirring until incorporated. Bring to a boil, then reduce to a simmer, stirring occasionally, until the sauce thickens. Add the shrimp and season to taste with salt and cayenne or white pepper. Divide the grits into four bowls, spoon the shrimp and sauce over the grits, garnish with the scallion greens, arugula, and crumbled bacon, and serve.

Simple Supper Shrimp and Grits

This is a constant in the Bass-Dupree household. Jack Bass cooks the shrimp, and Nathalie chops the garlic, tomatoes and basil. It takes 5 minutes for them to be finished. If you have a small family, cook at least 1 cup of grits at a time and freeze or refrigerate the unused portion in a plastic bag. Reheat in the microwave or over a very low heat with additional liquid if necessary.

2 cups cooked grits
4 tablespoons butter and/or olive oil
1 pound shrimp, peeled

1 medium tomato, chopped
1 to 2 garlic cloves, chopped
1 tablespoon julienned fresh basil or parsley

Reheat the grits in the microwave or over low heat, with additional liquid if necessary.

Melt the butter and/or olive oil in a saucepan, preferably non-stick. Add the shrimp and sauté until just before they turn pink. Add the tomato and stir until liquid exudes slightly, just a minute or so. Add the garlic and cook briefly.

Divide the grits between two plates, pour the shrimp and tomato mixture on top, garnish with basil or parsley and serve.

Variations: **Add 1 quarter-sized slice of chopped ginger to the pan with the garlic.**

Richmond Peppered Shrimp and Grits

Serves 2

Occasionally, I am sent very special recipes like this one, which combines a number of Southern ingredients with our beloved shrimp. Over the years, several students of mine have told me it is their favorite shrimp recipe. This dish can be prepared ahead and refrigerated, covered. Reheat quickly before serving.

2 cups cooked grits, cooked with shrimp stock
    or water
3 tablespoons butter
6 sliced scallions, green and white parts
    separated
1 tablespoon chopped fresh ginger
1 tablespoon soy sauce

1 tablespoon prepared horseradish
1/4 cup tomato sauce
1/2 teaspoon red pepper flakes
1 1/2 tablespoons peanut oil
1 pound large shrimp, peeled
Salt and freshly ground black pepper
Hot sauce

Stir the hot grits and butter to combine. Combine the white part of the scallions with the ginger, soy sauce, horseradish, tomato sauce, and red pepper flakes in a small bowl. Heat the oil in a large heavy-bottomed frying pan over medium-high heat. Add the scallion mixture and cook until the sauce is heated through. Add the shrimp and cook, stirring, until they turn pink, about 3 minutes. Season to taste with salt, pepper, and hot sauce. Divide the hot grits between two plates, spoon the shrimp over the grits, garnish with the sliced green scallion tops, and serve.

Spicy Shrimp with Oil and Garlic Grits

There are those who love anchovies and those who don't. If you love them, you will love this dish with its garlicky anchovy taste.

4 cups cooked grits
1/2 cup chopped Italian parsley, divided
2 pounds jumbo shrimp, peeled
Juice of 1 lemon
4 tablespoons chopped garlic, divided

Coarse salt
6 tablespoons extra-virgin olive oil, divided
1 teaspoon crushed red pepper flakes
1 (2-ounce) tin anchovies, drained

Mix the grits with 1/4 cup parsley. Toss the shrimp with the lemon juice, 2 tablespoons garlic, 1 teaspoon salt, and 2 tablespoons oil. Heat a large non-stick frying pan over medium-high heat. Working in batches, sauté the shrimp mixture for about 3 minutes, or until the shrimp turn pink. Remove the shrimp. Add the remaining oil, remaining garlic, red pepper flakes, and anchovies to the pan. Break up the anchovies with a fork and blend them into the oil. Add the remaining parsley and the grits and stir to mix well. Season to taste with salt. Divide the hot grits between four bowls, place the shrimp on top, and serve.

Grits "is" vs. Grits "are"

Grits, like the Italian polenta, is an "is," not an "are." We say, "Grits is good," just as we say "Polenta is good." They are kissin' cousins—both corn-based grinds—of different textures. They will vary according to the color of corn, whether yellow, white, or a mixture, and the method of grinding. They may be cooked and eaten as is, slathered with butter, or cooked and reheated in various ways: as delicate soufflés, casseroles, fritters, cut in shapes, dipped in cheese and fried, used as platforms for tomatoes or shrimp, breads, cookies, crackers, etc. They may be runny and used as a dip, or firm and used as a base for a heavier product like shrimp. They love eggs, bacon, cheese, hot peppers, sausage and, most of all, shrimp.

Red Curry and Pineapple Thai Shrimp and Grits

I got the idea for this recipe from James Peterson's wonderful book, *Fish and Shellfish*. I have, however, cut back considerably on the spiciness. Feel free to add more if you need fire coming from your mouth. Fresh pineapple is readily available cored and peeled.

4 cups cooked Lemon Grass Grits (see p. 114)
2 tablespoons butter
1 1/2 pounds large or extra-large shrimp, peeled
1 garlic clove, finely chopped
1 tablespoon finely chopped lemongrass,
   bottom part only*
1 tablespoon vegetable oil
2 kaffir lime leaves*

1 (14-ounce) can unsweetened coconut milk
1/2 to 3 tablespoons red curry paste*
3 tablespoons bottled Thai fish sauce (nam pla)*
1/4 cup fresh lime juice
2 cups fresh pineapple, cut into small wedges
   (about half a pineapple)
2 tablespoons finely chopped fresh cilantro
Salt and freshly ground black pepper

Stir the hot grits and butter to combine. Toss the shrimp with the garlic and lemongrass in a plastic bag and refrigerate for 2 hours. Heat the oil in a large non-stick sauté pan over high heat. Add the shrimp and toss or stir until they turn pink, about 2 minutes. Remove the shrimp.

Add the kaffir lime leaves, coconut milk, red curry paste to taste, fish sauce, and lime juice, making sure the curry paste is well stirred into the rest of the sauce. Bring the mixture back to a simmer, stir in the pineapple, cilantro, reserved shrimp and any juices. Bring to a simmer over high heat. Season to taste with salt and pepper. Serve over hot grits.

*Available in the Asian food section of most supermarkets. The lemongrass and kaffir lime leaves grow easily in Charleston and much of the lowcountry.

Putting on the Dog!

Cheese Grits Soufflé with Shrimp Sauce

Serves 8

A soufflé is just a thick sauce to which egg yolks and beaten egg whites are added. Cheese grits make a sturdy sauce base for the eggs, enabling the soufflé to be assembled in advance and cooked just before serving, or cooked and frozen. Top the servings with the Shrimp Sauce. This is an extraordinarily popular dish for a buffet.

FOR THE SOUFFLÈ:
4 cups cooked grits, cooked with milk
1 pound grated sharp cheddar cheese
1/2 cup butter
1 tablespoon Dijon mustard
1/8 teaspoon mace
1 teaspoon salt
1/4 teaspoon cayenne pepper
6 eggs, separated

FOR THE SHRIMP SAUCE:
1/4 pound butter
1 1/2 pounds small shrimp, peeled and deveined
1 1/2 tablespoons chopped fresh parsley
1 1/2 tablespoons chopped fresh basil

To make the soufflé: Preheat an oven to 350 degrees F. Generously butter an 8 1/2 by 13-inch oven-proof baking dish.

The grits should have the consistency of a sauce. If they are very thick, add more milk and heat until absorbed. Stir in the cheese, butter, mustard, mace, salt, and cayenne pepper. Cool slightly. Taste for seasoning and add more salt if desired.

Lightly beat the egg yolks in a small bowl. Stir 1/2 cup of the grits into the yolks to heat them slightly, then add the yolks to the grits mixture and combine thoroughly. Beat the egg whites until soft peaks form and fold into the grits. Pour into the baking dish. (The soufflé may be made several hours ahead to this point, covered and set aside or refrigerated. When ready to bake, return to room temperature.) Bake the soufflé for 40 to 45 minutes, or until it is puffed and lightly browned. Remove from the oven and cover lightly.

To make the shrimp sauce: Melt the butter in a large, heavy-bottomed frying pan. Add the shrimp and cook for 3 to 4 minutes, or until they turn pink. Add the chopped herbs and mix well.

Divide the soufflé among eight plates, ladle the shrimp and sauce over the grits, and serve.

Grits Roll Filled with Tomato Sauce, Shrimp and Mushrooms

Serves 6

The affinity of shrimp and grits is enhanced with this puffy flat cheese soufflé to which familiar pizza ingredients and shrimp have been added. Filled with a tomato sauce, shrimp, and mushrooms, it may be made ahead and reheated just before serving. It makes the splash of a soufflé—without the tension.

FOR THE GRITS ROLL:
1 cup cooked grits, cooked in milk
$2/3$ cup grated cheddar cheese or $1/3$ cup Swiss
    cheese and $1/3$ cup Parmesan cheese
4 egg yolks
Salt and freshly ground black pepper
6 egg whites

FOR THE FILLING:
1 cup sliced fresh mushrooms
4 tablespoons butter
$1 1/2$ cups cooked and peeled medium shrimp
3 cups tomato or marinara sauce
Salt and freshly ground black pepper
1 to 2 tablespoons fresh herbs (optional)

To make the grits roll: Preheat oven to 350 degrees F. Line a $10 1/2$ x $15 1/2$-inch jellyroll pan with a greased aluminum foil, parchment paper, or Silpat liner.

Combine the grits and cheese, and stir to melt the cheese. Lightly beat the egg yolks in a small bowl. Stir $1/2$ cup of the grits into the yolks to heat them slightly, then add the yolks to the grits mixture and combine thoroughly. Season to taste with salt and pepper.

Beat the egg whites until they stand in firm peaks. Fold $1/4$ cup of the egg whites into the grits mixture to soften, then fold the whole mixture into the remaining egg whites. Do not overwork or the whites will deflate. When all the egg whites are folded in, spread the mixture into the lined jellyroll pan. Smooth the top and bake 20 to 25 minutes, or until the top springs back lightly and a toothpick inserted comes out clean. Remove the pan from the oven and turn it upside down onto another piece of aluminum foil or parchment. Remove the pan. Strip off any pan liner from the grits.

To make the filling: While the grits roll is baking, cook the mushrooms lightly in the butter in a small frying pan until tender. Add the shrimp, cook until they turn pink. Remove from the heat. Heat the tomato sauce. Spread 2 cups over the interior of the grits roll. Distribute three-fourths of the mushroom and shrimp mixture over the tomato sauce, reserving the rest to garnish. Season to taste with salt and pepper. Roll the grits up like a jelly roll, beginning from a long side and, using foil, parchment, or Silpat to help flip it onto a platter. Slice the roll into six pieces. Serve with the remaining hot tomato sauce, garnish with the remaining mushrooms, shrimp, and herbs.

Goat Cheese, Basil and Shrimp Timbales

An adaptation of a recipe in *Southern Memories*, this is a simple but stunning dish for a summer garden party. It is particularly easy now that there are so many non-stick molds available in cookware stores. The timbales are best made just before serving, but the sauce can be made a day or two ahead. In the winter, you can usually find watercress; if not, use a good tomato sauce.

FOR THE TIMBALES:
2 cups cooked grits, cooked with half milk
   and half water
7 ounces goat cheese
1 egg, lightly beaten
2 tablespoons finely chopped fresh thyme
Salt and freshly ground black pepper

FOR THE BASIL SAUCE:
1/2 cup heavy cream
1/2 cup sour cream
2 bunches basil, sorrel, or watercress
1 1/2 pounds shrimp, peeled
2 tablespoons chopped basil, thyme, and/or oregano
Salt and white pepper

To make the timbales: Preheat an oven to 350 degrees F. Generously butter 6 (^{1}/2-cup) molds or ramekins.

Combine the grits and cheese, and stir to melt the cheese. Stir 2 tablespoons of the hot grits into the egg. Stir the egg back into the saucepan of grits. Stir in the thyme. Season to taste with salt and pepper. Spoon the grits into the prepared molds and place them in a large baking pan with sides. Add enough hot water to reach halfway up the sides of the molds. Bake for 30 minutes, or until a fork inserted in the center comes out clean. Remove from the oven.

To make the basil sauce: To make the sauce, add the heavy cream and the sour cream to a heavy-bottomed saucepan. Bring to a boil over medium-high heat, taking care that it does not boil over. Reduce the heat and simmer until reduced by about half, about 10 minutes. Meanwhile, wash and stem the basil, sorrel, or watercress, draining well. When the cream has reduced, add the herbs. Process in a food processor or blender until well puréed and smooth. Season to taste with salt and white pepper.

Cook the shrimp in gently boiling water until they turn pink, approximately 2 to 3 minutes. Drain. Toss with the basil, thyme, and/or oregano.

Unmold the warm timbales on six plates and spoon the sauce around them. Divide the shrimp between the plates and serve immediately.

Easter Saturday Shrimp and Grits

Mitchell Crosby and Randall Felkel always try to prepare something special on Easter Saturday and have guests over for a long luncheon. This recipe for shrimp and grits will be their 2006 appetizer.

FOR THE GRITS:
4 cups water
2 tablespoons butter
Salt
1 cup Hoppin' John's stone-ground grits
3 eggs, lightly beaten
2 tablespoons heavy cream
3 tablespoons crumbled crisp bacon

FOR THE SHRIMP:
2 tablespoons olive oil
1 tablespoon butter
1 1/4 pounds medium shrimp, peeled
3/4 cup gin
1/4 cup heavy cream
1 large leek, white part only, cut in 1/8 inch slices
2 tablespoons finely chopped fresh parsley
1/2 teaspoon black pepper

To make the grits: Per John Martin Taylor's (known as "Hoppin' John" Taylor) directions, bring the water, butter, and salt to a boil. Gradually add the grits, return to a boil, then reduce to a simmer. Cook the grits, stirring occasionally so that that they do not stick or form a skin, until they are creamy and done to your liking. It takes about 25 minutes. Remove from the stove.

Whisk together the eggs and cream. Stir in 1/2 cup of the hot grits. Whisk the egg and grits mixture back into the grits and blend well. Fold in the bacon. Pour the grits into a well-greased 9-inch cake pan. Cool to room temperature and refrigerate until the grits harden. Preheat an oven to 275 degrees F. Cut the grits into 8 triangles. Place them on a lightly-greased baking sheet and warm for 20 minutes.

To make the shrimp: Heat the oil and butter until bubbling. Sauté the shrimp until they turn pink, turning constantly. Add the gin, carefully ignite, and continue to sauté until the flame goes out. Remove the shrimp and cover lightly. Add the cream and leeks and cook for 3 to 4 minutes, or until the leeks are tender. Add the parsley and pepper.

Place 2 grits cake triangles on each of the four plates with their tips facing each other like a bow tie. Spoon the sauce and leeks around the cakes. Place the shrimp in the center of the bowtie and serve immediately.

Corn Timbales with Shrimp and Grits

Serves 12 as a starter

This recipe is adapted from one by Gary and Forsythia, a wonderful Atlanta catering company. Forsythia Chang was a shining star as a student at Rich's Cooking School. The addition of shrimp is mine. The timbales may be made a day or two ahead, carefully covered, and refrigerated.

3 cups cooked grits
1 cup grated sharp cheddar cheese
1/2 cup heavy cream
4 eggs, lightly beaten
2 cups corn kernels, lightly chopped

1/2 cup chopped chives or finely chopped scallions
2 tablespoons butter
Salt and freshly ground black pepper
24 medium shrimp, peeled

Preheat an oven to 350 degrees F. Grease 12 oven-proof molds or ramekins.

Mix the hot grits with the cheese and cream. Stir in the eggs, corn, and chives. Spoon into the molds or ramekins and place them in a baking pan with sides. Pour in hot water to come halfway up the outsides of the ramekins. Bake for 20 to 30 minutes, or until the timbales are set and a knife inserted into the center of the timbales comes out clean. Remove from the oven and the baking pan.

Heat the butter in a heavy-bottomed frying pan and sauté the shrimp for 3 minutes, or until they turn pink. Season to taste with salt and pepper. Gently run a knife around the edges of the timbales and unmold them onto twelve plates. Top with the shrimp and serve.

Saffron Grits and Shrimp Mediterranean-Style

Serves 6 to 8

Perfect for dazzling company, this combination of seafood and grits is a cross of Italian, Spanish and French flavorings, making a true Mediterranean dish with the flavor of bouillabaisse and the presentation of paella in an interesting combination with grits. Although there are a lot of ingredients, the whole dish takes little time to make. Feel free to substitute seafood to get the freshest available.

2 tablespoons olive oil
1 fennel bulb, thinly sliced, fronds reserved
1 yellow bell pepper, seeded and sliced
1 red bell pepper, seeded and sliced
3 Roma tomatoes, cut in small quarters
2 garlic cloves, chopped
1 cup dry white wine
1 cup shrimp stock or clam juice
1 teaspoon saffron

12 littleneck clams, cleaned
12 mussels, cleaned and debearded
24 large shrimp, peeled
1 tablespoon heavy cream
1 to 2 teaspoons Pernod or other anise-flavored liquor
1 cup kalamata olives, pitted
Salt and freshly ground black pepper
6 cups cooked Saffron Grits
1 (3- to 4-ounce) package fresh basil leaves, chopped

Heat the oil in a Dutch oven or deep frying pan. Add the fennel, peppers, tomatoes, and garlic and sauté for about 10 minutes, or until tender. Add the wine, stock, and saffron. Add the seafood. Bring to a boil, reduce the heat slightly, and cook for approximately 5 minutes, or until the clams and mussels open and the shrimp turn pink. Remove the seafood and boil the remaining liquid until only half is left. Add the cream. Boil again until it has the appearance of a light sauce. Add Pernod to taste and the olives and boil for 3 minutes. Return the seafood to the sauce and heat through. Season to taste with salt and pepper.

Place the hot grits in the middle of a serving platter and sprinkle with some of the basil. Scoop out the mussels, clams and shrimp and place around the grits. Drizzle the sauce with the vegetables on top and garnish the dish with as much of the basil as desired. Serve immediately.

Shrimp & Grits Eggs Benedict

Serves 4 to 6

My life changed when I realized that eggs could be poached ahead of time, refrigerated in cold water, and reheated in boiling water when dipped in the water with a slotted spoon. So, always make more poached eggs than you think you will need.

4 cups cooked grits
1 1/4 cups freshly grated Parmesan cheese
   (preferably Parmigiano-Reggiano), divided
White pepper
8 thin slices country ham
1 tablespoon butter

1 tablespoon vegetable oil
1/3 cup panko or all-purpose flour
1 1/2 cups heavy cream
1 pound large shrimp, peeled
1 pound steamed fresh asparagus
Salt and freshly ground black pepper8 poached eggs

Stir the hot grits with 3/4 cup Parmesan until the cheese melts. Season to taste with white pepper. Spread the grits into a buttered 11 x 7-inch baking dish. (Alternately, use a baking sheet to get thinner, but more, grits cakes.) Cool to room temperature, cover, and refrigerate for up to 2 days.

Preheat an oven to 250 degrees F.

Warm the sliced ham on a baking sheet in the oven. Heat the butter and oil in a heavy-bottomed non-stick frying pan over medium-low heat. Cut the grits into biscuit-size circles and lightly dredge them in the panko or flour. Cook them for 3 to 4 minutes on each side, or until golden. Keep warm in the oven.

Heat the cream in a heavy-bottom pan over medium heat. Add 1/2 cup Parmesan and stir until it melts. Add the shrimp and carefully cook until they turn pink. Season to taste with salt and white pepper.

Place two rounds of fried grits on each plate. Top with ham and a poached egg. Spoon the shrimp and cream over the eggs. Garnish with asparagus. Sprinkle lightly with salt, pepper, and the remaining Parmesan. Serve immediately.

Serves 6 to 8

This is nearly a tart, only baked in a larger pan so individual pieces can be cut into squares. It can be served as a lunch or supper dish, or cut smaller and served for appetizers. A store-bought crust works just fine.

1 piecrust dough
2 tablespoons unsalted butter
2/3 cup white vermouth or dry white wine
2 1/2 pounds peeled shrimp
10 eggs, lightly beaten
1 tablespoon salt
1 teaspoon freshly ground black pepper

1/4 cup tomato paste
4 cups heavy cream
1 cup cooked grits
1 cup chopped scallions, white and green parts
3/4 cup grated Swiss cheese
2 teaspoons finely chopped fresh tarragon

Preheat an oven to 350 degrees F. Flour a board or the counter. Roll the dough out into a rectangle and fit it in a 9 x 13-inch metal pan, leaving a slight overhang on the sides. Chill until firm.

Line the dough-lined pan with crumpled parchment paper or aluminum foil and add dried beans, rice, or pie weights to weigh down the bottom. Bake until the pastry is set and partially cooked, about 15 minutes. Remove the liner and weights and cool.

Melt the butter in a heavy-bottomed frying pan. Carefully add the vermouth to the butter and stir. Add the shrimp. Cook over medium-high heat for 2 to 3 minutes, or until the shrimp turn pink and the liquid is evaporated. Remove the pan from the heat. Beat the eggs, salt, pepper, and tomato paste in a bowl. Stir in the cream and the grits.

Spread the scallions over the partially baked crust and top with the shrimp. Pour the cream and egg mixture over the shrimp. Stir with a fork to make sure that the mixture is well incorporated into the shrimp, or the filling will cook in layers. Toss the cheese with the tarragon, and sprinkle over the tart, stirring a little with a fork to ensure that the cheese does not just sit on the top.

Bake the tart until the filling is firm around the edges and fairly firm in the center, about 45 to 50 minutes. The center will finish cooking as the tart cools. When the tart has settled and cooled slightly, cut into squares and serve.

Prosciutto and Tomato Shrimp and Grits

Serves 6 as a starter

This recipe is adapted from a recipe of Chris Hastings, whose Birmingham restaurant, Hot and Hot Fish Club, is famous. Chris used what he calls corn grits, but we've tested it with all kinds of grits and it doesn't matter what kind you use—you will have everyone wanting second helpings.

4 cups cooked grits cooked with chicken stock
3/4 cup heavy cream
1/2 cup butter
1/3 cup finely chopped shallots
1 large garlic clove, minced
2 pounds large shrimp, peeled
1/2 cup dry white wine

1 (14 1/2-ounce) can diced tomatoes in juice,
   drained and juice reserved
4 ounces prosciutto, cut into thin strips
   (about 1 cup), divided
1/4 cup chopped fresh parsley
1/4 cup chopped fresh chives
Salt and freshly ground black pepper

Mix the grits with the cream. Heat the butter in a large heavy-bottomed frying pan over medium-high heat. Add the shallots and garlic and sauté until tender, about 4 minutes. Add the shrimp and sauté for 2 minutes. Using a slotted spoon, transfer the shrimp to a large bowl. Add the white wine to the frying pan and boil until reduced to a glaze, about 5 minutes. Add the drained tomatoes and half the prosciutto and simmer until slightly thickened, about 2 minutes. Add the parsley, chives, and sautéed shrimp and simmer until shrimp turn pink, about 2 minutes. Thin the sauce with some of reserved tomato juices, if desired. It should be a little soupy. Season to taste with salt and pepper.

Divide the hot grits between six shallow bowls. Top each serving with the shrimp, spoon on the sauce, garnish with the remaining prosciutto, and serve.

Chefs' Recipes

Bob Waggoner's
Shrimp and Grits Charleston Grill Style

Executive Chef Bob Waggoner is the top toque at the plush restaurant in the Charleston Place hotel. Local ingredients and French technique are his signature.

FOR THE GRITS:
2 1/4 cups chicken stock
2 1/2 tablespoons unsalted butter
1/2 cup Charleston Grill stone-ground grits
1 to 2 cups heavy cream
Salt and white pepper
1 teaspoon finely chopped fresh lemon zest

FOR THE SHRIMP:
8 jumbo shrimp, peeled and deveined
Salt and white pepper
1 tablespoon olive oil
1 teaspoon chopped garlic
2 teaspoons chopped shallots
1 yellow tomato, peeled, seeded, and diced
1/2 cup dry white wine
1/4 cup heavy cream
1 tablespoon chopped basil, preferably Opal

To make the grits: Bring the chicken stock and butter to a boil in a heavy-bottomed saucepan. Stir in the grits and return to a boil. Reduce the heat, allowing the grits to cook for another 15 minutes at a low boil, or until the grits are thick and have absorbed most of the chicken stock. Stir occasionally to keep the grits from sticking. Add 1/2 cup heavy cream and reduce the heat, allowing the grits to cook slowly for another 10 minutes. As the liquid is absorbed, add more cream, cooking the grits until they are thick and full-bodied. Add salt and pepper to taste. Stir in lemon zest.

To make the shrimp sauce: Sprinkle the shrimp with salt and pepper on each side. Heat the oil in a large heavy-bottomed pan. Add the shrimp. Cook for 1 minute on each side and remove from the pan. Add the garlic and shallots and cook for 30 seconds. Add the tomato and the white wine. Continue to cook until the wine is reduced by half. Add the cream and cook until it reduces to a sauce consistency. Return the shrimp to the sauce and add the basil. Cook until the shrimp turn pink. Season to taste with salt and pepper.

Divide the grits between two bowls. Spoon the shrimp and sauce over the grits and serve immediately.

Carolina's
Cheese Grits with Creamy Shrimp and Andouille Sausage

Serves 6

Located in the former home of Perdita's, a landmark Charleston restaurant, Carolina's was one of the first Charleston restaurants to venture into New Southern cooking. Rose Durden, for many years Executive Chef at Carolina's, usually brings a hint of Asian flavor to her food, but she stayed true to Southern tradition in her shrimp and grits.

FOR THE GRITS:
8 cups milk
1 cup heavy cream
8 tablespoons butter
2 cups stone-ground yellow grits
1 cup grated cheddar cheese

FOR THE SHRIMP:
Olive oil
$^3/4$ pound Andouille sausage, halved and sliced
1 each red, yellow, and green bell pepper, julienned
6 cremini mushrooms, cleaned and sliced
6 shiitake mushrooms, cleaned and sliced
2 tablespoons Cajun seasoning
2 cups heavy cream
30 large shrimp, peeled and deveined
2 teaspoons minced chives

To make the grits: Combine the milk, cream, and butter in a heavy-bottomed saucepan over medium-low heat and bring to a simmer. Gradually whisk in the grits and stir until smooth. Continue cooking for about 1 hour, or until the grits are soft and velvety. Remove from the heat and stir in the cheese. Cover and keep warm.

To make the shrimp: Coat the bottom of a large, heavy-bottomed frying pan with oil. Heat the oil over medium-high heat, add the sausage, and sauté for 1 minute. Add the peppers and mushrooms and sauté until they begin to exude moisture. Add the Cajun seasoning and mix well to combine. Add the cream and briskly simmer to reduce by half. Add the shrimp and cook for 3 minutes, or until they turn pink.

Divide the grits between six plates and spoon the shrimp and sauce over them. Garnish with the chives and serve immediately.

Circa 1886's
⊰ Shrimp and Antebellum Grits ⊱

Serves 4

Circa 1886 is located in the carriage house of the beautiful Wentworth Mansion. Giving a nod to history, Executive Chef Marc Collins mixes Lowcountry cuisine with colonial influences and classic West Indian flavors.

FOR THE GRITS:
1 cup heavy cream
1 cup chicken stock
1 cup water
2 teaspoons Worcestershire sauce
1 teaspoon Tabasco
1 cup Anson Mills Antebellum Roasted grits
1/2 pound grated sharp white cheddar cheese
Salt and freshly ground black pepper

FOR THE SHRIMP:
1/4 pound applewood-smoked bacon, diced
3 tablespoons olive oil
32 large shrimp, peeled and deveined
1 large yellow onion, julienned
1 cup white wine
4 cups bottled clam juice
1/4 cup heavy cream
2 ounces demi-glace*
6 tablespoons cornstarch
2 tomatoes, quartered, seeded and julienned
1 bunch cilantro, stemmed and minced
Juice of 1 lime
Salt and freshly ground black pepper

To make the grits: Place the cream, stock, water, Worcestershire sauce, and Tabasco in a heavy-bottomed pot. Bring to a boil and add the grits. Stir constantly for the first 4 minutes. Reduce the heat to low and continue to cook until the grits are soft, stirring occasionally to keep the bottom from scorching. Add the cheese and stir until melted. Season with salt and pepper to taste. Remove from the heat and keep warm.

To make the shrimp: Put the bacon and oil in a heavy-bottomed frying pan. Cook over medium-high heat until the bacon browns, stirring constantly. Add the shrimp and stir, searing all sides, then remove and reserve. Add onion and sauté lightly. Deglaze the pan with wine. Add the clam juice, cream, and demi-glace and stir well. Bring the mixture to a simmer. Mix the cornstarch with just enough water to dissolve it. Slowly pour it into the pan, stirring until the mixture thickens. Add the shrimp to the sauce and cook until they turn pink. Remove from heat and fold in the tomatoes, cilantro, and lime juice. Season with salt and pepper.

Divide the grits between four plates. Spoon the shrimp mixture over the top and serve immediately.

*Demi-glace is made by reducing stock to a glaze. It can be purchased from gourmet food shops and through online catalogues. Reduced beef stock or the jus from a Sunday roast are possible substitutes.

Craig Deihl's
Fresh Hominy

Serves 4

Craig Deihl, Executive Chef of Charleston's Cypress Lowcountry Grille, has created a heritage food for his menu: freshly made hominy. He uses Anson Mills' yellow hominy corn, southern hardwood ash (either pecan, hickory, or oak) from his grill and smoker, and a time-honored process. This recipe makes 3 $^1/_2$ or 4 cups of hominy.

The first step in making hominy involves making lye. It is essential that no aluminum be used. The pots that the hominy is made in must be stainless steel or enamel-coated cast iron. The utensils must be either wood or stainless steel. The measuring cups should be glass. The cook should wear gloves. At this strength, the lye will not burn your skin, but it will cause discomfort.

The ratio of water to ash should be 2 to 1. Use 1 gallon water and 8 cups of ash. The mixture will be sludgy and wet.

Combine the water and ash in a large stainless or enamel-coated pot. Let this sit for at least a day. All of the soot will settle to the bottom. Strain. This will eliminate big pieces, but there will still be some ash in the water. Discard the pieces of ash.

Add this water to 2 pounds of dried yellow corn. The kernels will gradually turn from yellow-orange to grayish black, which indicates that the process is working. Cover and put in a cool place, but do not refrigerate. Let sit for at least a day.

A day later, begin to cook the kernels over low heat. Always keep at a simmer. There should never be any bubbles and the water should never be hotter than 180 degrees F. Stir every half hour. After 3 hours, start stirring the kernels every 5 minutes. The hulls should start popping off. As the mixture gets sludgy and thick, the skin starts to melt off the kernels.

When all of the hulls seem to be off, rinse the kernels well. It's important to get the hulls completely off. Return the kernels to the pot and add enough water to cover them $^1/_2$-inch. They will start to absorb fresh water. Cook over low heat until the kernels begin to soften. They should feel almost like a raw field pea. When the kernels start to puff up, rinse them again.

Return the kernels to the pot and add enough water to cover the kernels by $^1/_2$ inch. Add $^1/_4$ cup salt. Cook the kernels over low for about 30 minutes. Taste one every few minutes. When the kernels are done, they should be tender. Drain, rinse, and shock the kernels in ice water with some salt in it. Drain again. If you see any little hulls still, rub the kernel in your hands to break off every last bit of skin. Keeps refrigerated for up to 2 days.

Cypress Lowcountry Grille's
Seared Wahoo, Truffle Grits and Shrimp

Serves 2

Charleston's Cypress Lowcountry Grille is all about glamour, with its high-tech décor and 4,000-bottle wall of wine. Executive Chef Craig Deihl serves up an haute cuisine take on a Lowcountry staple.

FOR THE TRUFFLE GRITS:

3 cups water
1 cup stone-ground white grits
3 tablespoons butter
1/4 cup heavy cream
2 tablespoons truffle oil
1 1/2 tablespoons sea salt
1/2 teaspoon white pepper
1 1/2 tablespoons honey

FOR THE WAHOO AND SHRIMP:

1 (12-ounce) wahoo fillet, skin removed, cut in 2 pieces
Salt and freshly ground black pepper
2 ounces olive oil
10 tablespoons cold butter, divided
6 large local white shrimp, peeled and deveined
2 tablespoons thinly sliced garlic
3 tablespoons thinly sliced shallots
1 cup asparagus tips
3 ounces white wine
Juice of 1/2 lemon
1/2 cup grape tomatoes, sliced in half
3 tablespoons chopped fresh basil
1 teaspoon sea salt
Pinch of white pepper

To make truffle grits: Bring the water to a boil. Add the grits and cook them for 25 to 30 minutes over medium-low heat, stirring occasionally, or until the water is absorbed and the grits are slightly creamy. Stir in the butter, cream, truffle oil, sea salt, pepper, and honey and cook for another 10 minutes.

To make the wahoo and shrimp: Sprinkle the fish with salt and pepper. Heat the oil in a heavy-bottomed frying pan over medium-high heat. Add the fish to the pan. Sear the fillets for 2 to 3 minutes, turn them over, and add 4 tablespoons butter, the shrimp, garlic, and shallots. Continue to cook for 2 to 3 minutes. Remove the fish and shrimp from the pan and keep warm. Add the asparagus tips to the pan and cook for 1 to 2 minutes. Deglaze the pan with the white wine and gently boil the wine to reduce it by half. Reduce the heat to low. Stir in the remaining butter, tablespoon by tablespoon, until melted and creamy. Add the lemon juice, tomatoes, basil, salt, and pepper.

Divide the grits between two plates and top with the shrimp and then the Wahoo. Place equal amounts of the asparagus and tomato mixture on top of the fish, spoon the sauce around the fish, and serve immediately.

Craig Deihl's
"Nontraditional Shrimp and Grits"

Serves 4

Executive Chef Craig Deihl of Cypress Lowcountry Grille can always be counted on for a unique Asian spin on a conventional dish. Green grits? You won't believe how good this is.

FOR THE CILANTRO LIME GRITS:
6 1/2 cups water, divided
1 cup stone-ground grits
2 tablespoons sea salt
White pepper
1 bunch cilantro, stems removed
2 teaspoons sea salt
1 1/2 teaspoons white pepper
1/4 cup fresh lime juice
3 tablespoons honey

FOR THE BURNT ORANGE SAUCE:
3 oranges, cut into quarters
1/4 cup sugar
1 teaspoon sea salt
1/4 cup mirin (Japanese wine)
3 cups fresh orange juice
3/4 cup sugar
1/4 cup soy sauce
3 tablespoons nam pla (fish sauce)
2 teaspoons Sambal Oelek (Indonesian chile sauce)
Salt and freshly ground black pepper

To make the cilantro lime grits: Bring 3 cups water to a boil in a heavy-bottomed saucepan. Add the grits and cook for 35 to 40 minutes over medium-low heat, stirring occasionally, or until the water is absorbed and the grits are creamy and smooth. If needed, add a little water and mix until the desired consistency is reached. Add the salt and pepper to taste, remove from the heat, and keep warm. Bring 3 cups water to a boil. Blanch the cilantro in boiling water for 30 to 40 seconds, then plunge it into ice water. Remove the cilantro from the ice water and press all of the water out. Combine the blanched cilantro and the salt, pepper, lime juice, honey, and remaining water in a blender and purée until smooth. Strain the purée and add it to the grits. Season to taste and keep warm.

To make the orange sauce: Preheat an oven to 400 degrees F.

Coat the orange quarters with the sugar and salt, place them on a baking sheet with sides, and bake for 30 minutes, or until they get a dark caramel covered crust that almost looks burnt. Remove the orange quarters from the baking sheet and deglaze the baking sheet with the mirin. In a heavy-bottomed

(continued on page 92)

saucepan, combine the orange juice, sugar, soy sauce, nam pla, and Sambal Oelek with the burnt orange segments and deglazed liquid. Gently boil over medium heat until the volume is reduced by half, 15 to 20 minutes. Season to taste with salt and pepper, strain, and keep warm.

FOR THE SHRIMP:

1/4 cup peanut oil	*20 large white shrimp, peeled and deveined*
1/4 cup peeled and chopped fresh ginger	*1 recipe Burnt Orange Sauce*
1/4 cup chopped garlic	*1 tablespoon chopped fresh mint*
1 1/2 cups julienned leeks, washed well	*1 tablespoon chopped fresh cilantro*

To make the shrimp: Heat the peanut oil in a large heavy-bottomed frying pan over high heat. When it starts to lightly smoke, add the ginger and garlic. Sauté until golden in color, 2 to 3 minutes. Add the leeks and shrimp and cook for 3 to 4 minutes, or until the shrimp turn pink, moving the shrimp so they cook evenly. Add the Burnt Orange Sauce, mint, and cilantro, and mix well.

Divide the grits between four plates. Spoon the shrimp in the center of the grits, spoon the sauce on top, and serve immediately.

Frank Lee's
Sunday Night Shrimp and Grits

Serves 6 to 8

We tempted Slightly North of Broad's Executive Chef Frank Lee to tell us how he cooks his shrimp and grits at home. His official Southern Maverick Kitchens rendition follows his home recipe.

Small creek shrimp, peeled not deveined	*Fresh garlic*
Butter	*Salt and pepper to taste*

Sauté the shrimp in butter and fresh garlic. Season to taste with salt and pepper. Serve over stone-ground grits with a slice of tomato and Dixie Lee peas.

Maverick Southern Kitchens'
Shrimp and Grits

Serves 4 to 6

Executive Chef Frank Lee cooks up this shrimp and grits recipe for the Maverick Southern Kitchens restaurant, Slightly North of Broad. With great décor, lots of energy, and an open kitchen, SNOB serves up fun as well as good food.

FOR THE GRITS:

4 cups water
1/2 teaspoon salt
2 tablespoons unsalted butter, divided
1 cup stone-ground grits
1/4 cup heavy cream

FOR THE SHRIMP:

2 tablespoons unsalted butter, divided
1 1/2 links Kielbasa sausage, cut in 1/4 inch slices
4 ounces country ham, julienned
8 medium scallops
12 medium shrimp, peeled and deveined
2 tomatoes, peeled, seeded, and chopped
1/4 cup sliced scallions
1/4 teaspoon minced garlic
Pinch of Cajun seasoning
1/4 cup water
Salt and freshly ground black pepper

To make the grits: Combine the water, salt, and 1 tablespoon butter and bring to a boil in a heavy-bottomed saucepan. Slowly pour in the grits, stirring. Cover and cook over low heat, stirring frequently, for 1 hour, or until the grits are tender. Add the cream and remaining butter and remove from the heat.

To make the shrimp: Heat 1/2 tablespoon butter in a heavy-bottomed sauté pan over medium heat. Add the sausage and ham and sauté for 3 minutes, or until the ham is golden. Remove the sausage and ham and add another 1/2 tablespoon of butter. Increase the heat to medium-high, add the scallops and sauté them for 1 minute per side, or until golden. Remove the scallops and add another 1/2 tablespoon of butter. Add the shrimp and sauté them until they turn pink, about 3 minutes. Remove the shrimp and add the remaining butter.

Add the tomatoes, scallions, garlic, Cajun seasoning, and water and cook until heated through. Return the sausage, ham, and seafood to the pan and cook until heated through. Season to taste with salt and pepper.

Divide the grits between four plates, spoon the shrimp mixture over them, and serve immediately.

High Cotton's
Crab-Stuffed Shrimp with Grits, Collards, and Pepper Gravy

Serves 4

Executive Chef Jason Scholz mans the kitchen in this posh plantation-style restaurant. He featured this take on the opening menu, setting a high standard for High Cotton's creative cuisine.

THE GRITS:

6 cups water
8 tablespoons butter
2 cups heavy cream
2 cups stone-ground grits
Salt and freshly ground black pepper

THE STUFFING:

1 1/2 pounds bacon
1 pound claw crabmeat
1 red bell pepper, finely diced
1 green bell pepper, finely diced
1/2 red onion, finely diced
1 egg, lightly beaten
1/4 cup heavy cream
2 teaspoons prepared yellow mustard
1 tablespoon fresh lemon juice
6 dashes hot sauce
1/4 cup cracker meal (approximately) or 1/3 cup bread
   crumbs
1 pound large shrimp, peeled, deveined, and butterflied
Salt and freshly ground pepper

To make the grits: Bring the water, butter, and cream to a boil in a heavy-bottomed saucepan and pour in the grits, stirring. Simmer on low for 1 hour, stirring frequently, or until the grits are creamy. Season to taste with salt and pepper.

To make the stuffing: Precook the bacon until it is almost done, but still pliable. Drain on paper towels. Gently pick over the crabmeat to be sure there are no shells. Mix together the crabmeat, peppers, onion, egg, cream, mustard, lemon juice, and hot sauce. When thoroughly mixed, stir in cracker meal or bread crumbs until the mixture is dry enough that it doesn't easily cling to your hands. Season to taste with salt and pepper. Put a small amount of the crab mixture between the butterflied sides of the shrimp and wrap the shrimp with the bacon. Refrigerate.

FOR THE COLLARDS:
6 strips bacon
$1/2$ yellow onion, chopped
1 cup pepper vinegar, such as Texas Pete
1 bunch collard greens, washed, stemmed,
   and chopped
Salt and freshly ground black pepper

FOR THE GRAVY:
1 carrot, roughly chopped
4 ribs celery, roughly chopped
1 yellow onion, roughly chopped
8 tablespoons butter
1 teaspoon cracked black pepper
1 teaspoon salt
$1/2$ cup all-purpose flour
$1/4$ cup dry sherry
2 cups Shrimp Stock (see p. 36)
2 teaspoons chopped fresh parsley

To make the collards: Sauté the bacon and onion in a tall pot. When brown, add the pepper vinegar and boil for 5 minutes. Add the collard greens, cover the pot, and steam the collards until tender. You may need to add a little water to keep them from drying out. Season to taste with salt and pepper.

To make the gravy: Purée the carrot, celery, and onion in a food processor. Heat the butter in a heavy-bottomed frying pan over medium heat. Add the puréed vegetables, pepper, and salt. Sauté until tender. Sprinkle the flour over the vegetables and stir well. The mixture will become pasty. Continue to stir and cook for an additional 5 minutes. Add the sherry and shrimp stock. Bring to a boil. The mixture will thicken as it comes to a boil.

To serve: Preheat an oven to 400 degrees F. Place the shrimp on a baking sheet with sides and roast them until the bacon is crisp and the crabmeat filling is cooked. Divide the grits between four bowls. Top with collard greens and the shrimp. Lightly cover with the pepper gravy so there is an even, thin layer over the shrimp, collards and grits. Garnish with chopped parsley and serve.

Hominy Grill's
Pan-Fried Shrimp and Cheese Grits

Serves 4

Cutting his teeth in Bill Neal's kitchen set Robert Stehling's style. He delivers sophisticated Southern cuisine with surprising simplicity. It's all about the flavor. An added plus: Hominy Grill has the perfect patio for outdoor dining and lingering in the shade for a leisurely weekend brunch.

FOR THE CHEESE GRITS:
1 cup stone-ground grits
1 teaspoon salt
4 1/2 cups boiling water
3/4 cup grated sharp white Vermont
   cheddar cheese
1/4 cup freshly grated Parmesan cheese
3 tablespoons butter
Freshly ground black pepper
Tabasco

FOR THE SHRIMP:
3 slices bacon, chopped
2 tablespoons peanut oil
1 pound shrimp, peeled
All-purpose flour
1 1/4 cups sliced mushrooms
1 large garlic clove, finely chopped
Dash of Tabasco
2 teaspoons fresh lemon juice
Salt
1/4 cup thinly sliced scallions, green and white parts

To make the cheese grits: Whisk the grits and salt into the boiling water, reduce to simmer, and cook for 35 to 40 minutes, stirring frequently. When the grits are tender, turn off the heat and stir in the cheeses and butter until melted and combined. Season to taste with pepper and Tabasco.

To make the shrimp: Cook the chopped bacon in a large skillet until crisp. Set aside the bacon and pour off all but 1 tablespoon of the fat. Add the oil to the skillet and heat. Gently toss the shrimp with flour until they are lightly coated. Shake the shrimp to remove the excess flour.

Over medium heat, sauté the shrimp in the hot fat for 1 or 2 minutes until approximately half cooked. Add the mushrooms and toss. When they begin to cook, add the reserved bacon. Stir in the garlic. Very quickly add the Tabasco and lemon juice. Do not let the garlic brown. Season to taste with salt and add the scallions. The total cooking time is about 4 minutes, depending on the size of the shrimp.

Divide the hot grits between four plates, spoon the shrimp and sauce over the grits, and serve immediately.

FISH's
Grits Soufflés with Shrimp, Chorizo Cream Sauce and Bacon Tuile

Serves 4

Executive Chef Ryan Herrmann runs the show at this stylish Upper King Street restaurant crafted from an 1837 single house in Charleston, SC . This recipe, created by Sous Chef Sven Lindroth, typifies the au courant style of cuisine that you can expect when you dine at FISH.

FOR THE GRITS SOUFFLÉS:
2 cups stone-ground grits
8 cups cold water
2 cups heavy cream
8 tablespoons butter
6 eggs
Salt and freshly ground black pepper

FOR THE CHORIZO CREAM SAUCE:
2 tablespoons butter
1 tablespoon chopped garlic
1 tablespoon chopped shallots
4 ounces chorizo sausage, chopped fine
4 cups heavy cream
Salt and freshly ground black pepper

To make the grits soufflés: Preheat an oven to 350 degrees F.

Combine the grits, water, cream, and butter in a 3-quart stockpot. Bring to a boil, lower the heat, and simmer for 45 minutes, stirring occasionally, or until the grits are tender. Cool to room temperature.

Beat the eggs and fold them into the cooled grits. Season with salt and pepper. Pour mixture into 4 small greased soufflé cups and bake for 22 minutes, or until puffed and golden brown.

To make the chorizo cream sauce: Heat the butter in a heavy-bottomed saucepan. Add the garlic and shallots and sauté until translucent. Add the chopped chorizo and cook over medium heat for 3 minutes. Add the cream and cook until reduced by half. Season to taste with salt and pepper.

THE BACON TUILE:
2 (½ inch) wooden dowels
Heavy-duty aluminum foil
Non-stick vegetable spray
4 pieces bacon
Butcher's twine

THE SHRIMP:
2 tablespoons olive oil
1 cup chopped red bell peppers
1 cup chopped onion
1 tablespoon chopped garlic
24 large shrimp

To make the bacon tuile: Preheat an oven to 350 degrees F.

Wrap the dowels in aluminum foil. Spray the foil liberally with vegetable spray. Coil 2 slices of bacon around each dowel and tie with short pieces of butcher's twine. Place the dowels on aluminum foil-lined baking sheets with sides and bake in the oven for 10 minutes, or until cooked. The bacon must be fully cooked to stay curled. Remove the bacon from the dowels while still warm and allow to cool.

To make the shrimp: While the soufflés are in the oven, heat the oil in a heavy-bottomed frying pan and sauté the peppers, onion, and garlic until tender. Skewer the shrimp 3 to a skewer and grill until the shrimp turn pink.

Place a soufflé in the center of four plates. Balance 2 skewers of shrimp against it. Spoon a small amount of the sauce over the shrimp and onto the plate. Sprinkle with the pepper, onion, and garlic mixture. Garnish with a bacon tuile and serve immediately.

J. Bistro's
Creamy Cajun Ham, Shrimp and Grits

When he owned J. Bistro, James Burns brought a downtown-style dining destination to Mt. Pleasant, just north of Charleston. He dished up his creatively casual cuisine in contemporary digs. His rendition of this lowcountry favorite was a riff with New Orleans overtones.

2 tablespoons vegetable oil
2 teaspoons minced garlic
1/2 cup finely julienned country ham
1/4 cup diced celery
1/4 cup diced onion
1/4 cup diced green bell pepper
1 cup chopped tomato

2 tablespoons Paul Prudhomme's Cajun spice mix
1/4 cup white wine
1 1/2 cups heavy cream
1 1/2 pounds large shrimp, peeled and deveined
4 cups hot cooked stone-ground grits
1 bunch scallions, chopped

Heat the oil over medium heat in a large large heavy-bottomed frying pan. Sauté the garlic and ham lightly for 30 seconds. Add the rest of the vegetables, sprinkle in the Cajun spice, stir to combine, and sauté for 2 to 3 minutes.

Add the wine to the pan to deglaze it, scraping up any browned bits on the bottom of the pan. Add the cream and cook until the sauce is reduced and thickened to the desired consistency. If the sauce separates, whisk in more cream to bring it back together. Add the shrimp and simmer them in the sauce for 3 to 4 minutes, or until the shrimp turn pink.

Divide the hot grits between four bowls, spoon the shrimp and sauce over them, sprinkle with scallions, and serve immediately.

Jim Epper's
Shrimp and Grits with Country Ham and Red-Eye Gravy

Serves 6

Chef Jim Epper created this recipe at 101 Pitt in the Old Village of Mt. Pleasant. Now you'll find him steering the kitchen harbor-side as Executive Chef at Charleston's trendy Fleet Landing. Adding the Red-Eye Gravy gives the dish an interesting touch.

FOR THE RED-EYE GRAVY:
1 tablespoon butter
1 cup minced country ham
1/2 cup sliced cremini mushroom caps
1/4 cup minced shallots
1/2 cup Madeira
1/2 cup strong freshly brewed coffee
1 tablespoon cornstarch
1 (6-ounce) can spicy tomato juice
1 tablespoon minced fresh chives

FOR THE GRITS AND SHRIMP:
2 cups half-and-half
4 cups water
8 tablespoons butter
1 teaspoon salt
1 cup quick grits
1/3 cup grated sharp cheddar cheese
2 tablespoons butter
1 cup minced green bell pepper
2 pounds shrimp, peeled and deveined
1 teaspoon Old Bay seasoning
1/4 cup minced fresh parsley

To make the red-eye gravy: Heat the butter in a large heavy-bottomed frying pan over medium-high heat. Add the country ham and sauté until browned. Add the mushrooms and shallots and continue to brown. Add the Madeira and coffee and simmer for 15 minutes to reduce the liquid by half. Dissolve the cornstarch in the tomato juice and whisk into the sauce. Bring to a boil, stirring. Add the chives.

To make the grits and shrimp: Bring the half-and-half and water to a boil. Add the butter and salt. Slowly add the grits and reduce the heat. Cook the grits for 20 minutes, stirring frequently to keep from scorching. Fold in the cheese and stir to incorporate.

Heat the butter in a large heavy-bottomed frying pan over medium-high heat. Add the bell pepper, shrimp, and Old Bay seasoning. Sauté until the shrimp turn pink. Stir in the reserved Red-Eye Gravy and remove from heat as soon as the gravy has warmed.

Divide the grits between six plates, spoon the shrimp and gravy over them, sprinkle with parsley, and serve immediately.

Louis Osteen's
❧ "The Lowcountry's Finest Shrimp and Grits" ❧

Serves 6

Louis Osteen was one of the first local chefs to refine Lowcountry cooking. Charlestonians who miss his compelling cuisine can find it up the way at Louis's at Pawleys and its Fish Camp Bar. There's not a better reason for a road trip.

FOR THE GRITS:

2 cups milk
2 cups water
1 teaspoon salt
1 cup quick grits
4 tablespoons unsalted butter
1 cup heavy cream
2 teaspoons freshly ground black pepper

THE SHRIMP AND SAUCE:

6 slices bacon
1 cup finely chopped onion
1/3 cup finely chopped celery
1/2 cup finely chopped green bell pepper
2 teaspoons minced garlic
1 sprig fresh thyme or 1/4 teaspoon dried thyme
2 bay leaves
1/3 cup white vermouth or dry white wine
8 tablespoons all-purpose flour
4 cups Shrimp Stock (see p. 36), fish stock,
    or bottled clam juice
2 tablespoons tomato paste
2 cups heavy cream
Salt and freshly ground black pepper
Hot sauce (optional)
6 tablespoons butter
1 1/2 pounds medium shrimp, peeled

To make the grits: Bring the milk and water to a boil in a heavy-bottomed saucepan over medium heat. Stir in the salt. Slowly add the grits, stirring constantly. When the grits begin to thicken, turn the heat down to low and simmer for 30 to 40 minutes, stirring occasionally to prevent the grits from scorching. Stir in the butter and cream and simmer for 5 minutes. Stir in the pepper. Keep warm.

To make the shrimp and sauce: Cook the bacon until crisp in a large heavy-bottomed skillet over medium-high heat. Move to a paper towel to drain, reserving the fat in the skillet. Add the onion, celery, bell pepper, and garlic and sauté for 5 minutes. Add the thyme and the bay leaves and cook for 1 minute.

Increase the heat to high. Add the vermouth and cook 2 to 3 minutes, or until it evaporates. Lower the heat to medium and add the flour, stirring to prevent lumps. Be sure to scrape up any brown bits that are stuck to the bottom of the pan. Cook the flour for a few minutes to brown it, stirring constantly.

Add the stock and tomato paste. Mix quickly with a whisk to avoid lumps. When the mixture starts to bubble, add the cream. Return to a simmer. Season to taste with salt, pepper, and hot sauce. Slowly simmer the sauce for another 4 to 5 minutes while you cook the shrimp. Remove the bay leaves.

Using a cast iron skillet, melt the butter over medium-high heat. When the butter starts to bubble, add the shrimp and stir them until they are just about half cooked. Sprinkle with salt and pepper. Quickly pour the simmering sauce over the shrimp and cook for another 2 minutes, or until the shrimp turn pink.

Divide the grits between six bowls. Spoon the shrimp and sauce over the grits and garnish with the cooked bacon, either whole or chopped. Serve immediately.

Beach Water and Salt

"Beach water" is water gathered from coastal tributaries or from the faucets of those who live on the beach. There are restaurants whose claim to fame is that they cook their grits in beach water. They do not salt their water or their shrimp, both being salty enough, and hence are suspicious of anyone who automatically salts their water. Beach water has a mineral taste as well as a saltiness, and if pluff mud is there, the water will taste of it, too. Some think that salt will make their grits tough if added when they are cooking. Others insist on always adding it. It is hard to add salt after grits are cooked, so add it while cooking or just before the grits are removed from the heat.

Magnolias'
Pan-Fried Grits Cakes with Shrimp, Leeks, and Tomato Gravy

Serves 4

Executive Chef Donald Barickman's stellar Southern menu made Magnolias famous for more than its distinctive décor. This recipe is a star in his Uptown/Down South repertoire and in his second cookbook, *Magnolias: Authentic Southern Cuisine*.

FOR THE GRITS CAKES:
6 cups water
2 1/2 cups stone-ground grits
1 cup heavy cream
4 tablespoons butter
2 teaspoons salt
Pinch of white pepper

THE TOMATO GRAVY:
5 tablespoons butter, divided
3 tablespoons all-purpose flour
2 cups milk
2 ounces tomato juice
1 bay leaf
1 cup peeled, seeded, and diced fresh tomato
2 teaspoons salt
White pepper

To make the grits cakes: Bring the water to a boil in a heavy-bottomed stockpot or large saucepan. Slowly pour in the grits, stirring constantly. Reduce the heat to low and continue to stir so that the grits do not settle to the bottom and scorch. After 8 to 10 minutes, the grits will plump up. Cook the grits over low heat for 30 to 35 minutes, stirring frequently. The grits will have a thick, natural creamy consistency and become soft and silky. Stir in the cream, butter, salt, and pepper.

Pour the grits into a 9 x 13-inch pan. If you have to use a different pan, remember that the grits must be at least 1 1/4 inches thick. Cool to room temperature, cover, and refrigerate. When the grits have hardened, cut into the desired shapes, and reserve.

To make the Tomato Gravy: Melt 2 tablespoons butter without browning it. Whisk in the flour and cook over very low heat for 3 minutes, whisking. Add half the milk and whisk vigorously until the mixture becomes thick and is smooth. Add the rest of the milk and the tomato juice and whisk until the mixture thickens again. Add the bay leaf and tomato and cook over low to medium heat for 15 to 20 minutes, stirring frequently. Skim off any foam that may come to the surface and discard.

mixture thickens again. Add the bay leaf and tomato and cook over low to medium heat for 15 to 20 minutes, stirring frequently. Skim off any foam that may come to the surface and discard.

Cook the gravy over very low heat for 10 to 15 minutes more, stirring frequently. Season with salt and white pepper. Discard the bay leaf. Whisk in the remaining butter. Adjust the consistency of the gravy with water if it gets too thick.

FOR THE SHRIMP:

1 cup cornmeal for dusting
1/4 cup light olive oil
2 tablespoons butter
1 1/2 cups sliced leeks, washed well

1 pound medium shrimp, peeled and deveined
Salt and freshly ground black pepper
1/2 cup chopped fresh parsley

To finish: Dust the grits cakes with the cornmeal. Heat the oil over medium high-heat and pan-fry the grits cakes until they are golden brown on both sides and heated through. Only cook a few at the time so that the oil will stay hot and grits cakes won't stick. A heavy-bottomed non-stick skillet works well. Place onto paper towels and keep warm.

Heat the butter over medium heat and cook the leeks slowly, without browning, until tender. Add the shrimp. Cook until they turn pink. Season with salt and pepper to taste.

Place a grits cake on each plate and stack the leeks and shrimp on the cakes. Drizzle 3 tablespoons tomato gravy over and around them. Garnish with parsley and serve immediately.

Mike Lata's
Shrimp and Grits

Serves 4

Michael Lata cooked up this version of shrimp and grits when he was Executive Chef of Anson restaurant, where he was the first chef in Charleston to grind his own grits. Now he is co-owner and chef of FIG, a new Charleston favorite restaurant.

FOR THE GRITS:
2 cups milk
1 cup fresh white grits, such as Anson Mills
2 tablespoons unsalted butter
Salt and freshly ground black pepper

FOR THE SHRIMP:
2 tablespoons unsalted butter
2 tablespoons finely diced onion
2 tablespoons finely diced red bell pepper
2 ounces good country ham, finely diced
$1/2$ cup Shrimp Stock (see p. 36) or milk
$1/2$ cup heavy cream
1 pound medium shrimp, peeled and deveined
1 tablespoon snipped fresh chives
6 dashes of hot sauce
Salt and freshly ground black pepper

To make the grits: Bring the milk just up to a tiny boil around the edge of a heavy-bottomed non-stick saucepan over medium heat. Add the grits and stir for 1 minute. Turn the heat to very low. Skim the hulls, if any, from the surface with slotted spoon or sieve. Add the butter. Stir frequently for the first 10 minutes, then approximately every 10 minutes for 1 to 1 $1/2$ hours, adding more liquid if evaporation or absorption requires it, until the grits are tender. Cover them between stirrings to prevent evaporation. Remove from heat when creamy, and season to taste with salt and pepper.

To make the shrimp: Melt the butter in a large, heavy-bottomed frying pan. Add the onion and red pepper and cook until the onion is translucent, about 5 minutes. Add the ham and sauté briefly. Stir in the stock or milk. Scrape the sides and bottom of the pan to deglaze the pan, bring to a boil, and cook until the amount of liquid is reduced by half. Add the cream, bring to a boil, and reduce the liquid briefly, making a loose sauce. Add the shrimp, stir, and cook until the shrimp turn pink. Add the chives and season to taste with hot sauce, salt and pepper.

Divide the grits between four plates, spoon the shrimp and its sauce on top, and serve immediately.

The Old Post Office's
⊰ Fried Shrimp and Grits Skillet ⊱

Serves 2

Philip Bardin, Sous Chef Cherry Smalls, and Kitchen Manager/Assistant Sous Chef Bethany Fill-Pankey created this recipe especially for our book at Philip's very popular restaurant, The Old Post Office. It's down the coast on Edisto Island, but Charlestonians think that the drive is well worth it.

2 eggs, lightly beaten
1 cup buttermilk
1 tablespoon kosher salt
20 medium shrimp, peeled and deveined
1/2 cup all-purpose flour
1/2 cup cracker meal

1 tablespoon Old Bay seasoning
1 tablespoon butter
4 tablespoons olive oil
3 cups hot cooked whole-grain grits
1/2 cup grated cheddar cheese
1 lemon

Combine the eggs, buttermilk, and salt to make a bath. Soak the shrimp in this for 5 minutes. Combine the flour, cracker meal, and Old Bay Seasoning in a small bowl to make a breading. Dust the shrimp in the breading and let stand.

Heat the butter and oil in an 8-inch skillet over medium-high heat. Fry the shrimp for about 45 seconds on each side. Remove the shrimp and drain off all of the butter and oil.

Put the hot grits in the skillet and arrange the shrimp on top. Sprinkle on the cheese and melt it under a broiler. Finish with a squeeze of lemon and serve immediately.

Peninsula Grill's
Breakfast Shrimp and Grits with Andouille Sausage

Most people know about Executive Chef Robert Carter's divinely decorated dining room and deluxe dinner menu at Peninsula Grill in the Planter's Inn. What they don't know is that Inn guests also feast on breakfast there, enjoying Carter's good taste in the morning, too.

FOR THE GRITS:
3 1/2 cups water
2 tablespoons unsalted butter
1 cup heavy cream
2 teaspoons minced garlic
1 teaspoon kosher salt
1/4 teaspoon white pepper
1 cup stone-ground white grits
1 cup milk
1/4 cup grated Asiago cheese

FOR THE TOMATO JUS:
4 cups diced fresh tomatoes
1/4 cup diced celery
1/2 cup diced onion
1/4 cup peeled, diced carrots
1 teaspoon minced garlic
1 cup tomato juice
2 tablespoons chopped fresh basil
Salt and freshly ground black pepper
Hot sauce

To make the grits: Put the water, butter, cream, garlic, salt, and pepper in a heavy-bottomed medium-size saucepan and bring to a boil. Stir in the grits and bring back to a boil, stirring constantly. Reduce the heat to medium-low and simmer, stirring frequently, for about 20 minutes, or until the grits are tender. If the grits need more liquid, whisk in some of the milk. Fold in the cheese and set aside.

To make the tomato jus: Put the tomatoes, celery, onion, carrots, garlic, tomato juice, and basil in a heavy-bottomed medium-size saucepan. Bring to a boil, then reduce to a simmer. Simmer for 45 minutes. Purée in a blender, then strain through a medium-sized strainer. Season to taste with salt, pepper, and hot sauce.

FOR THE SHRIMP:
1 ounce clarified unsalted butter*
1/2 cup diced onion
1/2 cup diced Andouille sausage
24 large shrimp, peeled and deveined

1/2 cup diced tomato
3/4 cup Tomato Jus
1/4 cup chopped chives

To make the shrimp: Heat the butter in a large heavy-bottomed sauté pan over medium-high heat. Add the onion and sausage and sauté for 2 to 3 minutes, or until the onion is tender. Add the shrimp and diced tomato and sauté for 2 minutes. Add the tomato jus and simmer until the shrimp turn pink. Add the chives.

Divide the grits between four plates. Spoon the shrimp and sauce over them and serve immediately.

* To clarify butter, slowly melt it. The butter will separate into a layer of milk solids on the bottoms and a clear layer on top. Skim off any foam that may have formed and discard it. The clear layer is the clarified butter.

The Boathouse
Shrimp and Grits

Serves 4 to 6

There are few places that rival the waterfront view of The Boathouse at Breach Inlet, between Sullivans Island and Isle of Palms, SC. The restaurant overlooks both an Atlantic Ocean inlet and the Intracoastal Waterway. And few dishes compare with their signature shrimp and grits, topped with a decadent Hot Pepper Cream Sauce.

FOR THE HOT PEPPER CREAM SAUCE:
1/3 cup green Tabasco
1/4 cup dry white wine
1 shallot, chopped
1 tablespoon fresh lemon juice
1 tablespoon rice wine vinegar
1/2 cup heavy cream

FOR THE GRITS:
5 cups water
3 cups milk
1/2 cup heavy cream
8 tablespoons unsalted butter
2 cups yellow corn grits

To make the hot pepper cream sauce: Combine the Tabasco, wine, shallot, lemon juice, and vinegar in a heavy-bottomed medium-size saucepan. Boil over medium heat until the amount of liquid is reduced to 1/2 cup, about 15 minutes. Stir in the cream. Set aside.

To make the grits: Bring the water, milk, cream, and butter to a simmer in a medium-size heavy-bottomed pot. Gradually whisk in the grits. Stirring frequently, simmer the grits until they are soft and thickened, about 1 hour.

FOR THE SHRIMP:

$1/4$ cup olive oil

8 ounces Andouille sausage, sliced

1 red bell pepper, chopped

1 yellow bell pepper, chopped

$1/2$ cup minced onion

4 teaspoons chopped garlic

30 large shrimp, peeled and deveined

4 plum tomatoes, chopped

1 teaspoon Cajun seasoning

1 teaspoon Old Bay seasoning

Salt and freshly ground black pepper

To make the shrimp: Heat the oil in a heavy-bottomed medium-size frying pan over medium heat. Add the sausage, peppers, onion, and garlic and sauté until the vegetables are tender, about 8 minutes. Add the shrimp, tomatoes, Cajun seasoning, Old Bay seasoning, and sauté, stirring, until shrimp turn pink. Add salt and pepper to taste.

Divide the grits between the plates. Spoon the shrimp mixture over the grits. Drizzle warmed Hot Pepper Cream Sauce on top and serve immediately.

The Culinary Institute of Charleston's
Vermont White Cheddar Grits with Shrimp

Serves 4

Chef Ben Black is an instructor at the new, state-of-the-art Culinary Institute of Charleston, located at Trident Technical College. He delivers a Vermont Cheddar twist to a traditional rendition of Lowcountry shrimp and grits.

1 pound medium shrimp
1 tablespoon olive oil
1 tablespoon minced shallot
1/4 cup finely sliced red onion
1 teaspoon minced garlic
1/4 cup finely sliced yellow bell pepper

1/4 cup finely sliced red bell pepper
2 teaspoons Old Bay seasoning
White pepper
1 tablespoon heavy cream
4 cups cooked grits, combined with 4 ounces
    Vermont white cheddar cheese

Peel and devein the shrimp, saving the shells. Cover the peeled shrimp and refrigerate. Make a shrimp stock by placing the shrimp shells in a stockpot and covering with cold water. Cook over medium heat until the amount of liquid is reduced by half, about 20 minutes. Strain and discard the shrimp shells and keep the stock.

Place the oil in heavy-bottomed sauté pan. Add the shallot, onion, and garlic and sauté for 2 to 3 minutes, or until the vegetables are tender. Add the shrimp and bell peppers. Sauté until the shrimp turn pink. Add the Old Bay Seasoning and pepper to taste. Stir in the cream and 1 ounce of the shrimp stock.

Divide the grits between four plates, spoon the shrimp and sauce over them, and serve immediately.

Grits Alone

Microwave Grits with Cream and Cheese

Serves 4

Although you can do this recipe in a heavy pan on the stove, this is really an easy way to make decadently rich grits.

1 cup quick grits
4 cups heavy cream
2 to 3 tablespoons butter

Salt and freshly ground black pepper
$1/2$ cup freshly grated Parmesan, Swiss,
   or Monterey Jack cheese

Slowly stir the grits into the cream in a 6- to 8-cup glass bowl. Cook the grits according to their type, on 50 percent power. Stir occasionally, being careful they don't burn. If grits begin to separate and turn lumpy, add water to keep them creamy. If they form big lumps, push with a wooden spoon against the sides of the bowl to separate. When cooked to your satisfaction, remove from the microwave and season to taste with the butter, salt, and pepper, then stir in the cheese. Cover immediately to prevent a skin from forming. May be made ahead and reheated in the microwave.

Lemon Grass Grits

Serves 6 to 8

These have a particular affinity for Thai and Vietnamese recipes, adding a little underlying zing and flavor.

4 cups Lemon Grass Shrimp Stock (see p. 36)
1 cup uncooked grits
1 teaspoon salt

1 to 2 teaspoons very finely chopped lemon grass
1 slice ginger the size of a quarter, finely chopped
1 to 2 kaffir lime leaves

Strain the shrimp stock into a glass bowl for microwaving or a heavy-bottomed saucepan for cooking on the stove. Slowly stir in the grits. Add the salt, lemon grass, ginger, and lime leaves. Cook over low heat or microwave at full power until the grits are tender, adding more liquid if necessary. Remove from the heat and keep covered until used or cool to room temperature, cover, and refrigerate.

Grits with Yogurt and Herbs

Grits are good cooked in almost any liquid. For years they were cooked only in water, probably because it was available and not costly. Now they are cooked in a variety of liquids. I love them cooked with yogurt, but you might like to try them with sour cream or whipping cream or, even, mascarpone cheese.

3 cups plain yogurt
2 cups milk
1 cup quick grits
2 tablespoons butter

5 tablespoons chopped fresh lemon balm, thyme,
*   or mint (optional)*
1/2 cup heavy cream (optional)

Bring the yogurt and milk to a boil in a heavy-bottomed medium-sized saucepan. Stir in the grits slowly to avoid clumping. Cover and bring back to a boil. Cook as directed on the grits package. Stir frequently. If needed, add more liquid: yogurt, milk, or cream. When the grits are cooked, add butter, herbs, and optional cream. This dish may be made a couple of hours ahead and reheated in the same pan or in a microwave. Keep well covered with plastic wrap until reheating and serving time.

Grits Crisps

Leftover grits are very good to utilize for this recipe. These have many tasty uses, including accompanying soup, as a base for shrimp, tomato, and basil appetizers, and eating alone as a crispy treat.

1 cup cooked grits

1/3 cup freshly grated Parmesan, cheddar,
*   or Gruyere cheese*

Preheat an oven to 350 degrees F.

Take the cooked grits and press as them out as thinly as possible on a greased baking sheet. Chill until hardened. Cut out 1-inch rounds and move them to another greased baking sheet. Let come to room temperature. Top with the grated cheese and bake until crisp. Serve hot or cold.

Cheese Grits Casserole with Jalapeño Peppers

Perhaps the most popular of all grits dishes, with or without jalapeños, it is sturdy enough to travel, but creates the light impression of a soufflé. This goes well to church suppers, but it's also wonderful for brunch. It may be frozen and reheated, but it will lose its lovely puffiness.

4 cups hot grits, cooked in milk
1 pound white cheddar cheese, grated
1/2 cup butter
1/2 teaspoon ground mace
1 teaspoon salt

1/4 teaspoon cayenne pepper
2 to 3 garlic cloves, finely chopped
1/4 cup finely chopped jalapeño peppers (optional)
6 eggs

Preheat an oven to 350 degrees F. Butter a 2-quart casserole or 8 1/2 x 11-inch baking dish. Combine the hot grits, cheese, butter, mace, salt, cayenne pepper, garlic, and jalapeño peppers and stir well. Beat the eggs well, then add them into the grits mixture. Pour into the prepared dish and bake until set and lightly browned, 30 to 45 minutes.

Frittered Grits

You will love these little puffs, good to nibble on, good to float on soup, even good with confectioner's sugar sprinkled on.

1 package active dry yeast
1/2 cup water, 105 to 115 degrees F
1 teaspoon honey or sugar
1 teaspoon salt

1 cup cooked grits
1 egg, lightly beaten
1/4 cup flour
1 cup fresh lard or good vegetable oil

Dissolve the yeast in the water with the honey or sugar. Stir in the salt, grits, egg, and flour. Let sit several hours or cover and refrigerate overnight. Heat the fat or oil to 350 degrees F in a large frying pan. Drop spoonfuls of the fritter batter into the hot fat or oil, turning until brown on all sides. Serve immediately.

Serves 4 to 6

I can hear you now: How on earth did she decide to add rosemary to grits? Well, first of all, rosemary is abundant all over the South as a perennial bush, so it was handy. Next, corn loves rosemary, and many cornbreads are made with rosemary. It was just a short leap to grits with rosemary.

5 cups shrimp or chicken stock
1 cup grits
1 to 2 tablespoons chopped rosemary

1 tablespoon butter
Salt and freshly ground black pepper

Bring the stock to a boil and add the grits and rosemary. Cook 30 to 45 minutes, or according to package directions, until loosely cooked. Add the butter and season to taste with salt and pepper.

Variation: Rosemary shrimp with grits. Skewer shrimp on rosemary branches and grill. Serve on the grits. Add some pineapple if you like.

Peach and Grits Parfait

Kathleen Rogers, a brilliant graduate of Johnson & Wales culinary school, who was the food stylist for the pictures in this book, adapted this from a recipe that she found in *Food and Wine Magazine*. It can be made with any berry or soft-flesh fruit.

2 cups milk
1 vanilla bean
$1/2$ cup plus 2 tablespoons sugar
3 tablespoons unsalted butter
1 cup stone-ground grits
4 cups hot water
6 ripe peaches

FOR THE RASPBERRY SAUCE:
1 pint fresh raspberries or strawberries
$1/4$ cup sugar
$1/2$ teaspoon fresh lemon juice

Put the milk in a heavy-bottomed saucepan. Split the vanilla bean in half and scrape the seeds into the milk. Add the vanilla bean and sugar. Stir and bring to a simmer. Remove from heat and let stand for 30 minutes. Remove the vanilla bean.

Melt the butter in a large heavy-bottomed saucepan over medium-high heat. Add the grits and stir for 5 minutes. Whisk in the hot water. Reduce the heat to low and cook, stirring frequently, until the grits have thickened, 20 to 30 minutes. Reheat the milk and whisk it into the grits. Cook the grits over low heat, stirring frequently, until they thicken, about 20 to 30 more minutes. Remove from the heat, pour into a bowl, cool to room temperature, and refrigerate until chilled.

To make the sauce: Heat the ingredients in a heavy-bottomed saucepan, stirring occasionally, over medium-low heat until the berry juices flow and the mixture thickens. Remove from the heat, cool to room temperature, and refrigerate until chilled.

Slice the peaches right before assembling the parfaits. Layer fresh peach slices, grits, and raspberry sauce into parfait or wine glasses and serve.

Peach and Grits Cobbler

It's hard to believe that the traditional peach cobbler of the South, with a delicious batter that rises over the peaches, can be enhanced by grits. But enhanced it is. In both cases, the warm cobbler is wonderful topped with vanilla or peach ice cream.

1/2 cup butter
1 cup self-rising flour
1 cup sugar
1 cup milk

1/3 cup cooked grits
3 cups sliced fresh or frozen peaches, defrosted
1 to 2 tablespoons chopped candied ginger, optional

Preheat an oven to 350 degrees F.

Melt the butter in a 9 x 13-inch baking dish in the oven. Meanwhile, mix together the flour, sugar, milk, and grits. When the butter is melted, remove the baking dish from the oven and pour the flour batter over the hot melted butter. Mix the peaches and the candied ginger. Quickly spread the sliced peaches and their juices over the top of the batter. Return to the oven and bake until the sides are crisp and brown and the top is cooked, about 30 minutes.

Serves 4 to 6

Incredible in its tenderness, it tops rice pudding. It just melts in your mouth. If you have 2 cups dryly-cooked grits and would like to use them up, add 1 cup milk and stir thoroughly while heating through. Then you will proceed to add the rest of the ingredients and bake as directed below. This is good hot or chilled, with fruit or without.

$1/2$ cup cooked grits, cooked in 3 cups milk
2 tablespoons butter
$1/2$ cup sugar
2 cups heavy cream

4 eggs, beaten
1 teaspoon pure vanilla extract (optional)
1 tablespoon cinnamon (optional)

Preheat an oven to 325 degrees F.

Stir the loosely cooked grits with the butter. Remove from heat and cool slightly. Stir in the sugar, cream, eggs, and vanilla or cinnamon, if desired. Pour into a 4-cup buttered soufflé dish and bake until set and a knife comes out clean when inserted in the center, about 45 minutes. Do not worry if it becomes light brown on top and forms a skin, as this almost tastes like caramelized sugar, but don't let it burn or boil.

Once again, leftover cooked grits are put to good use. These waffles are surprisingly moist in the center, and nice and crisp on the outside. This is easier with a non-stick or well-seasoned waffle iron.

2 tablespoons melted butter plus butter
*   for the waffle iron*
$^1/2$ cup cooked, moist grits
2 cups flour

2 eggs
$^1/2$ teaspoon salt
1 teaspoon baking powder
1 cup milk

Brush the waffle iron with butter and heat. Beat together the ingredients in an electric mixer or food processor to make a batter. Add more milk, water, or cream if needed to make a thin batter. Spoon the batter into a very hot waffle iron, making sure it is spread evenly over the iron. Cover and cook according to the waffle iron's instructions. Remove, slather the hot waffles with molasses or maple syrup, and serve immediately.

Cinnamon-Raisin Grits Bread

Makes 1 loaf

I love this bread because I don't typically think of "sweet" things when making grits. If you love cinnamon-raisin bread, I suggest trying this bread for a little change. It's very nice for breakfast.

1 package active dry yeast
1 1/4 cups warm water, 105 to 115 degrees F
2 tablespoons honey
2 tablespoons butter, at room temperature
1 teaspoon salt
3 cups bread flour, divided
1/2 cup cooked grits
2 teaspoons cinnamon
1 cup raisins

GLAZE:
3/4 cup confectioner's sugar
1 to 2 tablespoons milk
1/2 teaspoon vanilla

Preheat an oven to 375 degrees F.

Dissolve the yeast in the water and stir in the honey. Separately, combine the butter, salt, 2 cups bread flour, and cooked grits in a large bowl. Add the dissolved yeast to the mixture and beat with a food processor or electric mixer for a minute or so. Turn out on a floured board and knead in the remaining flour, 1/2 cup at a time, until the dough is no longer sticky, but feels soft and tender. Move the dough to an oiled plastic bag and let it rise in a warm place until it has doubled in size, about 45 minutes.

Grease a loaf pan. Once the dough has doubled, punch it down and knead in the cinnamon and raisins. Form a loaf, move it into the loaf pan, and cover it with oiled plastic wrap to rise and double in size, about 30 minutes. Do not let the dough rise above the edge of the pan.

Bake for 30 to 45 minutes, or until an instant-read thermometer registers 190 degrees F when inserted through the center of the bread, or the bread sounds hollow when rapped on the bottom. Remove the bread from the pan and cool on a wire rack.

To make the glaze: Stir the sugar and milk until a smooth, spreadable consistency results. Stir in the vanilla and spread over the warm bread.

White Bread with Grits

Makes 1 round loaf

This white bread, made with bread flour and grits, has a very crisp crust that browns beautifully and has a very moist interior. It may be made by hand or with an electric mixer or sturdy food processor. Each will give the bread a slightly different texture, particularly the food processor, which chops the cooked grits and makes a more refined interior. No matter which way you fix it, you will agree that it will be one of the best breads you've ever made, and certainly one that is as good for toast as it is for bread. It's a wonderful use for leftover grits.

1 package active dry yeast
1 cup warm water, 105 to 115 degrees F
1 teaspoon honey

2 teaspoons salt
$^1/3$ cup cooked grits (preferably quick grits)
3 cups bread flour, divided

Dissolve the yeast with the water and honey in a large bowl. Stir in the salt, grits, and 2 cups bread flour, continuing to stir until you have a soft mixture that holds together. Turn the dough out onto the counter and knead 10 minutes by hand, or 10 minutes in a mixer, or a couple of minutes with a food processor, adding flour as needed. When it is thoroughly kneaded, place it in an oiled plastic bag to double in size, about 45 minutes. When doubled, remove from the bag, knock down, shape into a round and move to a baking sheet to double again.

Preheat an oven to 375 degrees F. When doubled in size, sprinkle with flour and bake for 30 minutes, or until an instant-read thermometer registers 190 degrees F when inserted through the center of the bread, or the bread sounds hollow when rapped on the bottom. Remove and cool on a wire rack.

Anadama Bread

Makes 2 loaves

My assistant, Ashley, converted this bread from cornmeal to grits, by grinding the grits further in the food processor until fine. She gives it as Christmas gifts.

1 package active dry yeast
1/2 teaspoon sugar
1/4 cup warm water, 105 to 115 degrees F
2 1/2 cups water
3 tablespoons butter, melted
1/2 cup molasses

1/2 cup stone-ground or quick grits, processed
  until fine
2 teaspoons salt
3 1/2 cups whole wheat flour
2 to 4 cups bread flour, divided

Dissolve the yeast with the sugar in the warm water. Mix together the 2 1/2 cups water, butter, and molasses in a heavy-bottomed saucepan. Stir in the grits and salt and bring to a boil. Set aside to cool.

Once the grits mixture has cooled to less than 115 degrees F, add it to the dissolved yeast. Move to a large bowl and stir in the whole wheat flour. Stir in 2 cups bread flour. Turn out onto a lightly floured surface and continue adding bread flour, 1/2 cup at a time, until the dough is no longer sticky and is smooth and elastic. The dough is ready when it bounces back after pressing it with a finger and feels like a baby's bottom. Form the dough into a round and let double in an oiled plastic bag, about 1 hour.

Grease two loaf pans. Punch down the dough and turn out onto a lightly floured surface. Knead lightly and divide in half. Shape each half into a loaf and put in the prepared loaf pans. Cover with oiled plastic wrap and let double in size again, about 30 to 45 minutes.

Preheat an oven to 400 degrees F. With a sharp knife, make three even slits on the top of each dough. Put the loaves in the oven and bake for 15 minutes. Reduce the temperature to 350 degrees F and bake for another 30 to 45 minutes, or until an instant-read thermometer registers 190 degrees F when inserted through the center. Remove the loaves from the pans and cool on a wire rack.

Fried Spicy Cheese Grits Pieces

Serves 8

This is a good use for leftover grits, and can be eaten like bread, as a snack, as a first course, or as a side dish. It's easy to make the base ahead and reheat later the same day.

3 garlic cloves, finely chopped
2/3 cup grated white extra sharp cheddar
* or Monterey Jack cheese*
1 jalapeño pepper, seeded and finely chopped
2 cups cooked grits

Salt and freshly ground black pepper
1/2 to 1 tablespoon hot sauce
4 tablespoons bacon drippings or peanut oil
1 egg, lightly beaten
1 cup bread crumbs

Butter an 8 x 8-inch pan or dish. Add the garlic, cheese, and jalapeño pepper to the grits. Season to taste with salt, pepper, and hot sauce. Spread in the pan and refrigerate until hardened. When ready to eat, heat the drippings or oil in a large heavy-bottomed frying pan. Cut the cold grits into squares. Dip the squares into the egg, coat with bread crumbs, fry until crisp on each side, 3 to 4 minutes, and serve.

Polenta and Grits

Historically, corn was a catch-all term for many grains, including references in Deuteronomy and in ancient Egypt; in the Colonies and England, "Guinney" or "Turkey wheate" were used similarly. Both polenta and grits originally meant "mush" in different languages; neither was a term for corn.

The Indians of the Americas introduced corn to the early explorers and showed them how to prepare it. Since the early settlers already ate porridges, they welcomed the strange corn and its child, grits (also spelled "gryts" and "grist").

By the time the colonists came to America, the Italians already had a highly developed cuisine using polenta. Which came first, then, polenta or grits? No one knows for sure, but Southerners don't want their grits called "Southern Polenta" and Italians don't want their polenta called "Italian grits." By the time the colonists came to America, the Italians had a highly developed cuisine using polenta. Polenta is a finer grind than grits, but many substitute one for the other in recipes.

Modern-day Southern grits owe a great deal to polenta and other corn preparations from all over the world. We have many ethnic recipes here, and we hope that you will enjoy cooking them!